Medieval Europe

Reader

ISBN: 978-1-68380-004-0

Medieval Europe

Table of Contents

Medieval Europe
Reader
Core Knowledge History and Geography™ 4

Chapter 1
Changing Times

Roads Lead to Rome You may have heard the expression, "All roads lead to Rome." During the glory days of the Roman **Empire**, that saying was true. Rome was the center of the empire, and roads from all over Europe led there.

The Big Question

What changes led to the decline of the Western Roman Empire?

Vocabulary

empire, n. a group of countries controlled by a single authority

These roads allowed the emperor to spread Roman ideas and laws throughout the vast empire. With the system of roads, the emperor could send messengers to carry instructions to the regional governors. Roads also allowed goods and taxes to travel across the empire into Rome. These goods and taxes kept the powerful Roman Empire running. More important, perhaps, was that Roman soldiers used the roads. Their job was to enforce the law and put down any rebellions or attacks on the empire.

Roads like this one in Italy were used to carry goods across the Roman Empire.

The roads helped hold the Roman Empire together, but they also played a role in its **decline**. Other armies could use these roads, too. The same roads that carried the Roman army out of Rome made it easy for outside **invaders** to march into the city. Beginning around 200 CE, some non-Roman groups of people wanted to do just that.

At this time, Rome was still a vast and powerful empire, but it faced some serious problems. Powerful Roman generals were fighting each other. Each general wanted to gain enough power to become emperor. This conflict was harmful for the health and well-being of the empire. The Roman government's main purpose was to provide law and order so that people could conduct business and live in safety. However, the fights among the generals undermined Roman law and order. The warring interrupted business, trade, and government.

> **Vocabulary**
>
> **decline,** n. gradual loss of importance and power
>
> **invader,** n. a person or group that comes into a country by force
>
> **boundary,** n. the edge of a country or of an area; its outside limits

In addition, this large empire needed money to build roads, bridges, and buildings, as well as to pay administrators and soldiers. Over time, it became impossible to pay for everything. Managing the Roman Empire well became impossible.

People on the Move

The Roman Empire grew weak enough in the 200s and 300s that it began to attract the attention of various groups that lived on the edges of the empire, or outside its **boundaries**. Rome had conquered some of these groups of people and had sent armies to guard the borders against others.

The Romans, who mostly spoke Greek and Latin, looked down on these people who spoke different languages and had different cultures. They labeled them "barbarians." The word *barbarian* comes from a Greek word meaning foreigner. The Romans dismissed these non-Greek- and non-Latin-speaking barbarians as primitive, **uncultured**, and inferior. However, many barbarian groups were not **uncivilized**. For example, many had skilled metal workers who created beautiful art, jewelry and coins.

The Romans referred to a number of groups as barbarians, including the Angles, the Saxons, the Huns, the Vandals, and the Goths (including the Ostrogoths and the Visigoths). Several of these groups of people were Germanic. They lived in northern Europe. The Angles and the Saxons lived in what is now Denmark and northern Germany. They eventually drove the Romans out of England. The Goths and Vandals attacked and eventually **sacked** the city of Rome itself. From the Roman point of view, the Vandals caused so much destruction that, even today, we still use the word *vandalism* to describe acts of destruction.

> **Vocabulary**
>
> **uncultured,** adj. showing poor manners and bad taste; crude
>
> **uncivilized,** adj. not advanced socially or culturally
>
> **sack,** v. to destroy and steal things in a city or building, usually with an army

However, the barbarians who left the longest memory of fear and destruction were not Germanic people. They were a nomadic people from central Asia called the Huns. The Huns lived on the

Barbarian Invasions of the Roman Empire

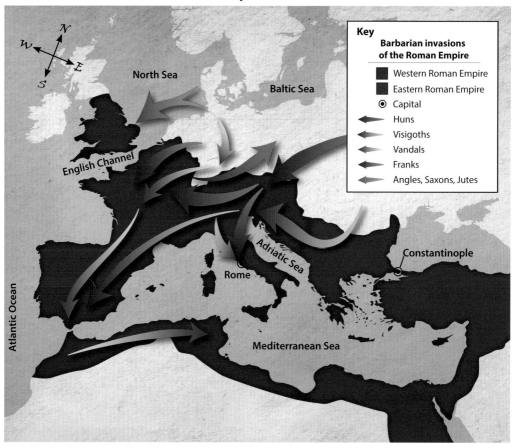

At its height, the Roman Empire covered parts of Europe, Africa, and Asia. Over time, non-Roman groups seized Roman lands. The beige area shows lands outside its boundaries.

steppe, a flat, grassy, treeless area that stretched across what is now Ukraine, southern Russia, and Kazakhstan.

The Huns raised sheep, cattle, and horses on the steppe. As the seasons changed, and the available grasses dried up, the groups moved in search of new grazing lands for their livestock.

The Huns were skilled horsemen and experts with bows and arrows. As young children, they learned to ride horses. So good was their horsemanship that one Roman historian described the Huns this way: "They are unable to put their feet on the ground. They live and sleep on their horses."

In the 300s, the Huns, tired of trying to survive on the steppe, began to move westward across Europe. Thanks to their skill in warfare and their excellent horsemanship, the Huns easily conquered other groups of people and moved onto their land.

Attila the Hun

The Huns struck fear into the hearts of those they challenged. The most feared of all the barbarians was Attila the Hun. For about ten years, Attila and his brother Bleda shared the throne as rulers of the Huns. But Attila wanted to rule alone. He killed his brother and became the sole king and leader of the Huns.

Attila became known as a brilliant but cruel general. He led the Huns westward, conquering other groups and leaving a trail of destruction. The Huns crossed the Danube River and crushed a Roman army in eastern Europe. Then they invaded what is present-day France. At one point, a Roman army joined with another barbarian group, the Visigoths, to defeat the Huns in a bloody battle in Gaul (present-day France). But that didn't stop Attila. It was to be his only defeat.

Next, Attila turned his attention to Rome itself. In 452, he swept across northern Italy. In an attempt to save Rome, Pope Leo I, the bishop of Rome, rode out to meet with the feared Hun general. Most Romans thought that was the last they would see of Pope Leo. But, as the legend goes, in a dramatic face-to-face meeting, Attila thought he saw a halo above the pope's head. The Church believed that Attila retreated because he feared this holy man, who seemed to have a power the cruel conqueror knew nothing about. Modern historians note, however, that Attila's forces were very weak at this point. Attila may also have been aware that Roman armies were approaching from the east. Regardless of the reasons, Attila decided not to attack Rome. Soon after this meeting, Attila became sick and died. Without their leader, and weakened by disease, the Huns retreated into eastern Europe.

This painting shows Pope Leo I (left), protected by angels, meeting Attila (right), who is on the black horse.

The End of the Roman Empire

You may have heard the expression, "Rome wasn't built in a day." It means that it takes a long time to accomplish a big task. It took hundreds of years before the Roman Empire reached its peak, and then it lasted for hundreds of years more. Eventually, the Roman Empire was split into two parts—the Western Roman Empire centered in Rome and the Eastern Roman Empire ruled from Constantinople.

Finally, in 476, a German king named Odoacer (/oe*doh*ae*ser/) attacked Rome and killed the emperor. Since no new emperor was named, the date 476 is sometimes used to mark the end of the Western Roman Empire. The Eastern Roman Empire, which was not conquered, lasted for almost another thousand years.

Chapter 2
The Not-So-Dark Ages

Life as Usual Today, we usually say that the Middle Ages began in 476, when the western half of the Roman Empire collapsed. However, to the people of the time, especially those who lived outside the Roman capital, there probably wasn't any difference between life in 475 and 477.

The Big Question

What problems arose as a result of not having a central government?

Even though the Roman government ceased to exist, day-to-day life went on as before for most people. People living far from Rome probably did not even hear about the barbarians or the fall of Rome. And even in areas where the barbarians took over, life remained more or less unchanged. Many of the barbarians respected Roman ways. As a result, the language and the structure of society remained the same. Religions, customs, and laws did not change all at once, either. People kept doing the things they had always done. For most people, their main concern was that law and order be preserved, and that they were able to feed themselves and their families.

Even after the collapse of the Roman Empire, Roman culture was much admired. This mosaic from Roman Britain most likely shows the Roman goddess Venus.

Gradual Change

Little by little, however, things did begin to change. Many Roman roads and **aqueducts** that were used to carry people, goods, and water began to fall apart. Although there were many local governments, there was no longer a central government with money to fix the roads. Even if a ruler in one region decided to repair the roads that crossed his land, there was no guarantee that the roads in the neighboring regions would be fixed, too.

The Romans were skilled builders. This aqueduct still stands over the River Gard in France.

Over time, **trade** declined in northern Europe. During the time of the Roman Empire, there had been lively trade among the northern outposts in Europe and northern Africa, as well as the eastern Mediterranean regions. Those northern European networks gradually stopped working. From around 600, it was nearly impossible for these regions to sell goods to northern Africa or to the eastern Mediterranean.

With the decline of trade, cities also began to shrink. **Merchants** sought new items closer to home to trade. The governors who had once carried out Roman laws were gone. Without stores and government offices, there were fewer jobs in the cities.

Most people survived by farming or soldiering. Without a central government to pay for big public buildings or ships, **artisans** couldn't practice their skills. Today, we have many books that explain how to do different things. Back then, few people could read or write. Usually skills were passed from an older

> ### Vocabulary
>
> **trade,** n. buying and selling goods among different peoples
>
> **merchant,** n. a person who buys and sells goods to earn money
>
> **artisan,** n. a person with a certain skill in making things

In the Middle Ages, most people survived by farming.

skilled worker to a younger worker. When the skills were no longer used and passed on, people often forgot them.

The Dark Ages

Because people forgot, or no longer used certain skills that were known by the Greeks and Romans, this period from about 500 to 800 was once called the Dark Ages. Was the term Dark Ages accurate? Well, not really!

> **Vocabulary**
>
> **scholar,** n. a person with special knowledge about a subject

The term was introduced by writers and **scholars** during the period in history that followed the Middle Ages. This period is known as the Renaissance. These writers gave their own accounts of what happened during the Middle Ages. They looked down on the Middle Ages as a time when there was no learning, so they called these years the Dark Ages. For a long time, people accepted what the Renaissance writers said about the Middle Ages.

Today, historians present a more balanced view, admitting the shortcomings of the Middle Ages but also noting its strengths. It is true that some valuable skills were forgotten during this time. Because travel was difficult and sometimes dangerous, most people stayed in their own areas. The Middle Ages also had its fair share of violence. However, today historians agree that the Middle Ages was probably not any more violent than the time of the Roman Empire, or the Renaissance. Modern historians see these years as a time of change and growth, contributing to the rise of Western civilization in many ways.

Spreading Out

In the years following the fall of Rome, nations that would greatly influence a changing Europe were slowly being created.

Remember the destructive Visigoths who sacked Rome? They continued to move westward, into present-day France. Then they crossed the Pyrenees Mountains and moved into Spain and Portugal, where they settled into a life of farming. The Ostrogoths moved into the area of central Europe that is now the Czech Republic and Hungary. The Huns were absorbed by other ethnic groups. The Angles and Saxons moved across the sea to England, whose name comes from the Angles—"Angle-land."

History is a little bit like a cake. Many ingredients go into it—and something very different comes out. In these years, the groups of people who brought down the Roman Empire began the process of creating a new and different Europe.

Chapter 3
Two Churches

The Bishop of Rome Although the city of Rome was much smaller after the fall of the Western Roman Empire, it was still a city. People living in the city needed food and other supplies.

The Big Question

Why did the collapse of the Western Roman Empire make it possible for the bishop of Rome to become more powerful?

It is very difficult for people who live in cities to grow the food they need. Food has to come from farming areas outside the city. After the fall of the empire, however, there was no one to take charge and arrange to bring these kinds of supplies into Rome. Who would perform those duties now?

Vocabulary

bishop, n. a high-ranking member of the church in some Christian religions

Remember when Attila the Hun almost attacked Rome? The person who talked him out of doing that was Pope Leo I, Rome's **bishop**. The term *pope* is another title given to the bishop of Rome. There was still an emperor at that time, but the power of the emperor was fading fast. The power of Rome's bishop, on the other hand, was growing.

Popes in the Middle Ages, such as Pope Gregory I, shown here, often had a lot of power.

The Victors Convert

Many Germanic groups conquered the Roman lands. And yet, in a sense, the **victors** had also been conquered. They weren't conquered by the Roman army, but by the Roman church. Rome was a **Christian** empire when it fell in 476, and many of the people who took Rome's lands eventually **converted** to Christianity. They also adopted Rome's **customs**, or traditions. Many also began to speak the language of Rome. Over time, the Roman language in the different parts of the old empire began to develop into different but related languages. That is why modern French, Italian, and Spanish are called Romance languages. These languages developed from the Latin language of Rome over hundreds of years.

Even though newcomers had conquered Rome, they admired what it stood for. It had been the center of the most powerful empire for hundreds of years. Rome's conquerors respected and held on to many Roman laws and customs. They also kept the Latin language and the Roman religion.

Vocabulary

victor, n. a person who defeats an opponent or enemy; winner

Christian, adj. related to beliefs based on the teachings of Jesus of Nazareth

convert, v. to change religious beliefs; to switch from one religion to another

custom, n. a tradition, or way of doing something, that belongs to a particular society, place, or time

Roman letters on a tomb

Romulus Augustus, the last emperor of Rome, surrendered to the German king Odoacer in 476.

When there was no longer a western emperor, the bishop of Rome became the most important official in the city. Pope Leo said that the bishop of Rome was the most important official in the Christian Church. He claimed that his power as bishop of Rome reached far beyond the city of Rome itself.

What were the reasons behind Leo's claim to power? He claimed that the power of the bishop of Rome came from Jesus himself, through Saint Peter. Leo said that Jesus chose Peter to be the head of the Church. According to Christian belief, Peter left Jerusalem after Jesus was killed and went to Rome. Leo and his supporters believed that Peter became the first bishop of Rome. The bishops of Rome that followed him were **heirs** to Peter's position as head of the Christian Church.

Using this argument, Leo and those who followed him claimed that they were the *papa* (from which we get the word *pope*), or father, of the Christian Church. With the former Western Roman Empire broken up into many smaller kingdoms and territories, the bishop of Rome, as leader of the Church in *all* these regions, claimed power throughout Europe.

Notre-Dame Cathedral in Paris was built in the 1100s. It is a fine example of Gothic architecture, which became popular in the Western Church of the Middle Ages. It is also a symbol of the power of the Church in the Middle Ages.

The Eastern Empire

Not everyone agreed with the claims of the bishops of Rome. In fact, there were four other bishops who also viewed themselves as leaders of the Christian Church. These were the bishops of Constantinople, Alexandria, Antioch, and Jerusalem. These cities were all located in the Eastern Roman Empire.

Remember how the Roman Empire was divided into two parts? One part was the Western Roman Empire, centered in Rome. The other part was the Eastern Roman Empire, also known as the Byzantine Empire. In the early 300s, Emperor Constantine, the first Christian emperor of the Roman Empire, built a new eastern capital at the site of the ancient Greek city of Byzantium. He named this new capital Constantinople. While the Western Empire was weakened by internal problems and eventually destroyed by invaders, the Eastern Empire survived.

However, the Eastern Empire's culture was much less Roman than the Western Empire's. The eastern part of the empire was more Greek than Roman. Most of its people did not speak Latin or languages that were influenced by Latin. Do you think the bishops of Alexandria, Antioch, and Jerusalem were more influenced by the bishop of Constantinople or by the bishop of Rome?

If you said Constantinople, you were right. Over time, the number of differences between Christians in the eastern and western regions increased. There had always been some differences, of course. Even though both groups were Christians, they spoke different languages and had different cultures. However, more and more disagreements sprang up. Some of these disagreements may seem trivial today, but in the Middle Ages they were not. For example, Christians in the former Western Empire used flat bread made without yeast in their **holy ceremonies**.

Vocabulary

"holy ceremony," (phrase), a religious act or ritual performed according to tradition

Christians in the Eastern Empire used bread made with yeast in their holy ceremonies.

More important was the larger issue of who was in charge of the Church. Bishops in the Eastern Empire did not like accepting the rule of the bishop of Rome as the final word on *all* Church matters. They were used to ruling in a more cooperative manner, in which each bishop had a vote.

Over time the bishops in the Eastern Church developed a very different tradition of governing the Church and its religious customs. They did, however, accept the belief that the bishop of

Rome was the heir of Saint Peter.

In 1054, the differences between the bishops of Rome and Constantinople came to a head. After some major disagreements, the two churches separated.

Hagia Sophia, the Church of the Holy Wisdom, was built in the 500s in Constantinople as the main cathedral for the Eastern Empire.

Two Separate Churches

Christian bishops in the Eastern Empire, including Bulgarians, Serbs, Russians, Syrians, and Egyptians, chose to join with the bishop of Constantinople. People on both sides of this argument expected that the division between the two parts of the Church was just temporary.

Over time, however, the two sides did not get back together. In fact, they found more reasons to disagree. Today, the Church that is headed by the bishop of Rome (the pope) is known as the Roman Catholic Church. The Church in the region that was ruled by Constantinople (now Istanbul, Turkey,) is generally known as the Eastern Orthodox Church. In the rest of this unit, we will mostly focus on the lands of the Western Church.

Split Between the Eastern and Western Churches

At the time, most people thought that the conflict between the two parts of the Church would be resolved.

Chapter 4
Prayer and Work

Saint Benedict of Nursia Just about the time of the fall of the Western Roman Empire, a boy named Bennet was born in the mountain village of Nursia, northeast of Rome. He was a very serious child who thought a lot about right and wrong. He was described as having "the mind of an old man" in a young man's body.

The Big Question

How did Saint Benedict's ideas help people in Europe during the Middle Ages?

The Abbey of Sant'Antimo near Siena, Italy, followed the rules of Saint Benedict.

Bennet's parents sent him to Rome to study, but the lying, cheating, and dishonesty he saw in the city upset him. He left Rome and decided to live as a **monk**, devoting himself to a religious life. At that time there were many monks in Asia, but there were very few of them in Europe.

The European monks who did exist lived isolated from the world—alone and away from all other people. They denied themselves the comforts of life for religious reasons. Many of them did things that were harsh and painful to themselves. They went without food, or lived in a cave for years on end. That is what Bennet did at first. He spent three years living in a cave by himself.

Eventually, Bennet, now called Benedict, decided that it was not enough to pray alone in a cave. He believed that monks should serve God *and* people. Gradually Benedict became known as a holy man. A group

Benedict's good works and holiness made him one of the most important saints of the Catholic Church.

of rich and influential monks invited him to become the leader of a **monastery**. Benedict accepted, but things did not go very well. When Benedict tried to get the other monks to serve God by helping other

people, they refused. The situation became so hostile that some of the monks even tried to poison Benedict.

Benedict saw that to put his new ideas into practice, he would have to start his own monastery. He moved to the town of Monte Cassino and wrote a book that is known today as the *Rule of Saint Benedict*. This book contains a list of rules to be followed in the monastery. Benedict did not ask people to seek holiness by going without food and water. Instead, Benedict asked monks to find God in ordinary, simple, and useful work. Work was balanced with prayer and reading, sleeping, and eating. He also emphasized the importance of working together, and getting along with everyone else in the monastery.

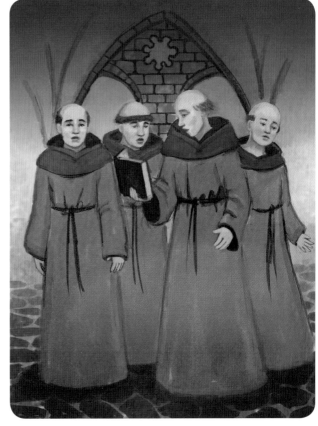

Medieval monks (and nuns) spent a lot of time praying. They also composed beautiful music and hymns.

Self-Sufficient and Hard-Working

Monte Cassino was a successful monastery, and Benedict's fame spread. Soon other monasteries were created to follow his rules.

Monasteries following Saint Benedict's rules were called Benedictine monasteries. These monasteries tried to be self-sufficient. That means that the monks grew and made almost

Monks grew their own food and made wine and beer.

everything they needed for themselves. They had gardens in which they raised their own vegetables. They kept chickens and goats to provide eggs and milk. They made cheese. They also baked their own bread, sewed their own clothing, brewed beer, and made wine.

Does it seem strange that these deeply religious people drank beer and wine? This is a good example of how customs change over time. In the Middle Ages, almost everyone drank small amounts of beer every day. Beer was considered a healthy drink because of the grains used to make it. There was usually just one meal a day, with a cold snack in the evening. Meals consisted of bread with eggs, cheese, or fish. The monks ate at assigned places. There was no conversation during the meals, but one monk read aloud from the **Scriptures**, or other religious books.

Benedict also asked monks to follow a shared schedule. When the bell rang for prayer, everyone in the monastery stopped whatever he was doing and went to the church.

A day in the monastery was divided into three general work periods. Monks spent about six hours in prayer and six hours doing manual work such as gardening, cooking, or sewing. About four hours were spent studying and writing. Monks slept seven to eight hours a night. Saint Benedict's rules are interesting to read in today's busy times.

The **abbot** made the rules in the monastery, and all monks had to obey him. Monks were required to show hospitality to all guests, whether invited or not. They had to treat all the monastery's possessions—whether gardening tools or precious altar pieces—with great care.

> **Vocabulary**
>
> **scripture,** n. the sacred writings of a religion
>
> **abbot,** n. the leader of a monastery
>
> **convent,** n. a community of nuns, or women who live a simple, religious life

Missionaries, Hospitals, Schools, and Libraries

The *Rule of Saint Benedict* had a great influence not only on Benedictine monasteries but also on other types of monasteries that developed later. This influence extended to **convents** and therefore to nuns, too. All together these religious institutions had a great impact on Europe's history.

Monasteries took on the role of supplying **missionaries** to spread Christianity. Saint Benedict himself was a missionary. Perhaps one of the most famous missionaries was Saint Patrick, who brought the Christian religion to Ireland. Saint Augustine of Canterbury, another famous missionary, brought Christianity to the Anglo-Saxons of Britain. Saint Boniface converted many groups of people in what is now Germany.

Young boys and girls trained from an early age to become monks and nuns.

During this time, governments provided little or no help for poor people. Saint Benedict believed that each monastery should offer help to the poor and needy. Thanks to him, over time, more help came from the Church. Monks and nuns ran hospitals for the poor and schools for children to train to become monks and nuns. Priests, monks, and nuns demonstrated that caring for the poor was part of their Christian duty.

Works of Art

One of the most important things that monasteries and convents did was to set up libraries. In the early Middle Ages, books were rare and expensive. Some people went their whole lives without ever seeing a book. Every book that had been written was copied by hand! Although there were important Islamic libraries in Asia and Africa, in Europe almost all the libraries that existed were in monasteries.

Monks worked long hours, often by candlelight, copying ancient texts. Most of the texts they copied were much longer than the book you are reading now. Think of how long it would take you to copy every word in this book by hand! Monks didn't just copy the words, either. They also decorated the first letters of important words

Knowledge was kept alive by monks, who would spend lots of time copying books for monastery libraries.

and the borders of their **manuscripts**, and they produced beautiful illustrations. Today, these handwritten books from the Middle Ages are considered valuable works of art.

Nearly all the manuscripts from the early Middle Ages were written in Latin. Even after the fall of the Roman Empire, Latin remained the official written language in Europe. Any document that had religious, legal, or scholarly significance was written in Latin.

For the most part, the only people who knew how to read and write during this time were priests, monks, and nuns. This was largely because the only schools that existed were religious schools. And most of the students there were in training for a religious career. People learned about the Bible from listening to a priest, monk, or nun.

Instead of books, information was passed along in different ways. Most people learned by watching and doing. Children would watch their parents make things, take care of animals, and farm. They grew up learning to do these things. Eventually they would get married and pass on these skills to their own children. For more skilled crafts, such as shoe-making and barrel-making, young men would work alongside master artisans to learn their craft.

Reading was an important activity in many monasteries and convents, but few people sat and read silently to themselves. Most of the time one person would read aloud to a group. If people wanted to make an oath, it was considered more important to say it out loud than to write it down and sign it.

Monasteries and convents still exist in the modern world, and monks and nuns continue the work they have done for more than a thousand years. Today, however, there are thousands of schools, universities, hospitals, and libraries all over the world. It may be hard to imagine how important the work of the Benedictine monasteries was to the lives of Europeans. But, for hundreds of years, monks and nuns were the teachers, writers, librarians, book publishers, doctors, and nurses for all of Europe.

Chapter 5
Charlemagne

A Head Above the Others Monks and monasteries spread Christianity through much of what was Europe. In the late 700s, however, one man would come along who was not a monk but who would do more than any other person to spread Christianity and strengthen the Western Church.

The Big Question

Why did King Charles earn the title Charles the Great, or *Charlemagne*?

That man was Charles, the king of the Franks. The Franks were a group of people who lived along the Rhine River in present-day Germany. Charles was not just the king: he might have also been the tallest man in his kingdom. Charles was six feet, three and a half inches tall. (We know that because his bones have been measured.) Even by today's standards, that is tall. But in the 700s, when people were shorter, he was *really* tall.

Charlemagne's people, the Franks, lived near the Rhine River.

Charles was not only tall, he was healthy and energetic as well. He followed health advice you've probably heard all your life! He ate healthy foods, exercised every day (he loved to swim), and got plenty of rest (he liked to nap). He was a hard worker, too. He started having meetings the minute he got out of bed, before he had finished dressing. His advisors would come into his bedroom and ask him questions.

This illustration shows Charlemagne as a powerful ruler.

Charles's greatest talent was organizing and **managing** people. He knew how to inspire armies to fight, and he also knew how to move them quickly from one place to another. This was an important skill for a leader in a time when there were no reliable maps. He didn't give up either. Once he started something, he finished it. He expected the same of his men.

> **Vocabulary**
>
> **manage,** v. to lead and direct; to run something, such as a project or business

Charles enjoyed being king. Like most rulers, he enjoyed the power of ruling. But unlike some kings, he had goals beyond gaining power for himself. He wanted to spread Christianity, and he encouraged learning. These goals, and Charles's ability to make things happen, combined to make him one of the greatest rulers Europe had ever known. Charles became so great that the "great" became part of his name. By the time he died, people were calling him *Charlemagne* (/shar*lə*maen/). Charlemagne means Charles the Great, and that is what historians today call him.

To the Rescue

The Frankish army was an impressive sight. Strong and disciplined, they wore leather vests and light armor. Their most important weapons were their swords, and Frankish soldiers treated their swords with care. Many of them had cases for their swords, called scabbards, decorated with silver, gold, and even jewels.

The Frankish army was very successful in battle. These strong soldiers with their glittering weapons conquered much of the territory that had once been part of the Western Roman Empire. The Moors, or Muslim North Africans, controlled most of the Iberian Peninsula, including Spain and Portugal. However, Charlemagne took parts of northern Spain, as well as most of what is now France, Germany, Switzerland, the Netherlands, Belgium, and Luxembourg. He united them into a Frankish empire. He had successes in northern Italy, too.

You have already read about how the bishop of Rome, also known as the pope, tried to gain more power after the fall of the Western Roman Empire. You have also read that the bishops of Constantinople, Alexandria, Antioch, and Jerusalem didn't like that very much. Well, Pope Leo III had enemies even closer to home. Powerful princes from the lands around Rome grew jealous of the Church's wealth and power. The pope's enemies actually attacked him as he was walking through the streets of Rome! They pushed him to the ground, pulled off his robes, and beat him.

The pope fled Rome and appealed to Charlemagne for help. Charlemagne did not let the pope down. He sent an army to escort the pope back to Rome, where his soldiers punished the pope's enemies.

The following year, Charlemagne went to Rome for two purposes. He wanted to make sure the pope was safe from any more attacks, and he wanted to celebrate Christmas with the pope. It was the year 800, the beginning of a new century, and Charlemagne wanted to celebrate this special year with the pope in Saint Peter's Church.

Emperor of the Romans

The celebration proved to be even more special than Charlemagne had dreamed possible. According to one of Charlemagne's biographers, Charlemagne prepared for a traditional Christmas **Mass**. When he arrived at the **cathedral**, he found it packed with people from all over his empire. His children were there, too.

> **Vocabulary**
>
> **Mass,** n. the name for the religious ceremony in which Catholics celebrate their relationship with God
>
> **cathedral,** n. the bishop's church; any large and important church

When Charlemagne reached the front of the cathedral, he knelt in prayer. After a long time he stood up, and the pope placed a crown on Charlemagne's head. The people in the church cheered. "Long life and victory to Charles Augustus,

crowned by God, great and peaceful emperor of the Romans," they cried.

Reading this today, it is hard to believe that Charlemagne was surprised by being crowned by the pope. But that's the story that has come down through the ages.

The crowning of Charlemagne as emperor accomplished three things. First, it gave the Romans an emperor for the first time since 476. Second, it gave Charlemagne the **blessing** of the pope. And, lastly, it established that Charlemagne agreed that the pope had the power to crown an emperor.

A Great Ruler

Charlemagne expanded his empire through warfare. However, what made him great wasn't what he did on the battlefield, but rather the way he governed his empire.

Charlemagne built a beautiful capital city Aachen (/ah*ken/), in what is now northwestern Germany. He built a palace and a chapel. He also had a great library. He started a school in his palace and allowed the sons of poor people to attend as well as

In 800, Pope Leo III crowned Charlemagne emperor of the Romans.

the children of nobles. Charlemagne believed that women should be educated as well as men, an unusual view for his time. He even tried to provide free education for his subjects.

Charlemagne was a good **manager** in times of peace as well as in war. He improved communication and organization throughout his empire. He sent teams of ambassadors chosen for their good character to enforce laws and solve conflicts in various parts of his empire. Like the Romans, he built roads and bridges to make trade and travel easier.

> **Vocabulary**
>
> **manager,** n. a person who leads and directs something, such as a project or business

When Charlemagne first began conquering the Saxons and other groups of people, long before he became emperor, he tried to force them to become Christians. At first, his rule was very harsh. People who would not convert to Christianity were killed. Later in his life, however, Charlemagne realized that force was not the best way to win people over. By the 790s, he allowed his conquered subjects to make their own choices about Christianity.

Charlemagne died in 814. None of the rulers who followed had his gift for leadership. However, Charlemagne set a new standard for learning and management. He helped shape what would later become some of the modern countries of Europe.

The Franks originally spoke an early form of German. By the time Charlemagne died, many Franks were speaking a new language that was influenced by Latin. This language became known (to English speakers) as French. Over the next 200 to 300 years, the French-speaking part of Charlemagne's empire broke away to form the kingdom of France.

Charlemagne's Empire

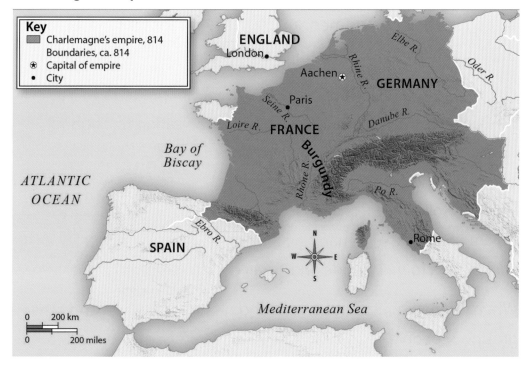

Charlemagne ruled areas that would become part of modern Europe.

The Holy Roman Empire

Charlemagne's empire continued in various forms for hundreds of years. Part of it expanded toward the east. It still included Rome, however, and a strong **alliance** remained between the pope and the rulers of this German-speaking empire.

In the 1200s, the Hapsburg family took control of this German empire. It was at this point that it became known as the Holy Roman Empire, having been blessed by the pope. This empire stretched roughly from the North Sea and the Baltic Sea in the north to the Mediterranean Sea in the south, and from the Rhone River in the west to beyond the Oder River in the east.

> **Vocabulary**
>
> **alliance,** n. a partnership of different countries, organizations, or people who agree to work together

Chapter 6
A Feudal Society

A New Society Who do you think is the most important person in your town or state? In every society there are certain people who are more powerful and influential than others.

The Big Question

How did the feudal system hold people, communities, and kingdoms together?

In the Middle Ages, they didn't have elections the way modern democracies do today. The important people in the Middle Ages were those who controlled land. These were the kings, **lords**, and **knights** who fought for the kings. Therefore, the people close to the king, especially the **nobility**, were the ones who had the most important jobs. The system that developed around the most powerful people is called **feudalism**.

> **Vocabulary**
>
> **lord,** n. a person with power and influence who controls land given to him by a king
>
> **knight,** n. a soldier on horseback who serves a king or other ruler
>
> **nobility,** n. powerful families that held fiefs and titles
>
> **feudalism,** n. a system of government in which land is exchanged for loyalty and services

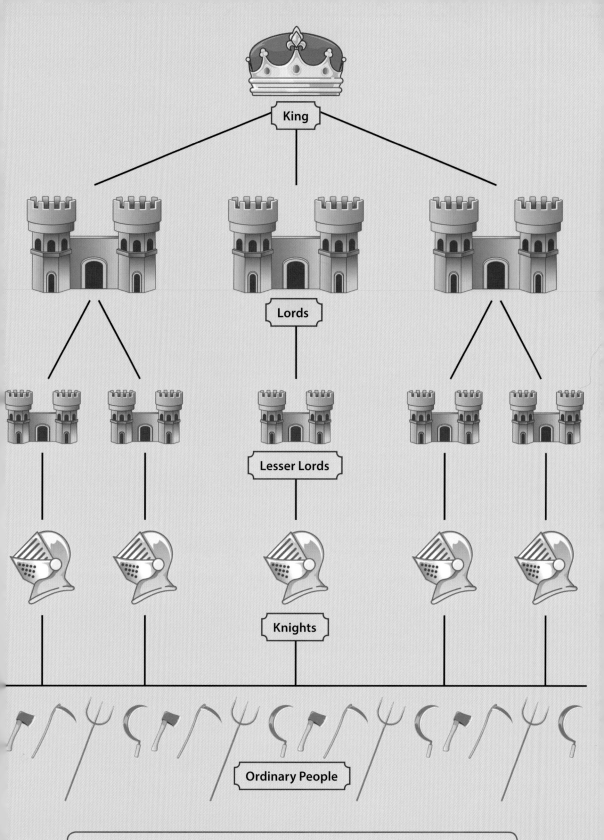

King

Lords

Lesser Lords

Knights

Ordinary People

Feudal society was based on a system of loyalty among all in the kingdom.

A Special System

Feudalism appeared first in Charlemagne's time. Over time, it gradually spread across **medieval** Europe. Feudalism arose because kings often needed warriors to fight for them. These kings made deals with powerful leaders, or lords. A lord would become a king's **vassal**. The king would give him a large amount of land, called a **fief**. And each would make certain promises to the other. The vassal would swear to fight loyally for the king. In return, the king promised to protect and support the vassal.

> **Vocabulary**
>
> **medieval,** adj. relating to the Middle Ages in Europe
>
> **vassal,** n. a person who receives land from a ruler and in return promises to fight for the ruler
>
> **fief,** n. a plot of land exchanged for loyalty to a ruler

Feudal government was not like our modern government. During the Middle Ages there were no nations or central governments in the modern sense. Instead there were networks of lords and vassals under the rule of a king. And, the promises, or oaths, that vassals swore were what held these networks together. The links between vassals and lords encouraged people to think of themselves as part of a larger whole.

Feudal agreements were meant to last. These agreements were made public with special ceremonies held in a church and arranged by kings and priests. The ceremony in which a man became a vassal was called an act of homage (/oh*mij/). **Homage** is the French word for honor or respect. Let's time-travel back to the Middle Ages and watch as a medieval lord pays homage to a king.

Kiss of Peace

Imagine being in a cathedral lit by hundreds of flickering candles. There are beautiful windows of stained glass and paintings and sculptures. The altar is made of carefully carved wood. Sitting in the cathedral are all the great lords of the kingdom and their families. They are dressed in their finest robes and jewels. At the front stands the king, waiting to receive his vassal.

A lord walks slowly down the center aisle of the cathedral. When he reaches the king, he falls to his knees and swears an oath. He promises to love and serve the king forever.

KING & KNIGHT.

A lord would fall to his knees and promise loyalty to a king.

The king then raises the kneeling man to his feet and announces that he is giving land to the lord. This is in exchange for the lord's promise of loyalty and other services. The king kisses his new vassal on the cheek in a "kiss of peace."

But feudalism was more than just the relationship between the king and his lords. The king's lords would also divide up part of their land and grant fiefs to vassals of their own. For example, the king's lords would grant portions of their land to lesser lords and to other soldiers called knights.

Feudal Government

Feudal loyalties held law and order in place within a kingdom. But there were few laws shared across different kingdoms. Individual lords made their own laws and enforced them in their own fiefs. The one law that extended across Europe was the sacred oath of loyalty that a vassal took. If a vassal failed to serve his lord or betrayed his lord, he became an outlaw, shunned and persecuted by other lords.

Over the years these noble titles and arrangements were inherited. This means that they were handed down from father to son. For example, if a father were a duke, earl, baron, count, or marquis, his son might get that title when the father died. The families who held fiefs became the nobility of central and western Europe. As nobles, they had special privileges that other people did not have. In this book, you will learn how feudalism in the Middle Ages provided a way for people to make a living. Feudalism also created a culture of knights, battles, and honor that is still remembered today.

King Richard II knighting his lords

Chapter 7
To the Manor Born

A Self-Sufficient Village You might be wondering what happened to the land that the vassals received from their lords. You probably know enough about dukes and counts and other nobles to guess that they weren't out milking cows and planting crops.

The Big Question

What kinds of jobs were serfs required to do on the manor estate?

Vocabulary

self-sufficient, adj. needing no help from others to live or survive

A manor house, a church, a mill, serfs' houses, and fields were all part of a typical manor estate in the Middle Ages.

On the other hand, there were plenty of people living during the Middle Ages who needed to eat but who did not receive fiefs from a king.

In much of northern Europe, each lord lived in a castle or **manor** house. The manor house was usually surrounded by the land where the food was grown and where the people who worked in the fields lived. The manor **estate**, as it was called, was a lot like a **village**. Nearly everything that people needed was grown or made there. In addition to their food, people who lived on the estate made their own soap, candles, furniture, leather, tools, and cloth. Most of the people who lived on the estate farmed. There were also some skilled workers, such as blacksmiths who made metal tools, horseshoes, and even swords.

In addition to the manor house for the lord, and cottages for the people who lived on the estate, there was usually a church. Sunday worship, baptisms, weddings, and funerals were held there. Next to the manor church there would probably be a graveyard where people from the estate were buried when they died.

Exchanging Labor for Land

The lord of the manor allowed **serfs**, farmers who were bound to the lord's land, to use his land. The serfs grew food on the land, kept animals that grazed on the land, and used the wood from the forests. The lord provided a mill to grind the grain grown on the manor, and large community ovens for baking the grain into bread. The lord also provided farming equipment such as plows and wagons, and teams of oxen to pull the plows and wagons.

The lord of the manor had other responsibilities, too. The lord provided the serfs with law and order. The lord had the authority to make important decisions. He also had the right to punish a serf caught committing a crime. In addition, a serf could not leave the estate he or she lived on, nor could he or she marry without the lord's approval. Only the king and the law of the Church could limit the lord's powers.

The lord also protected the people who lived on the manor estate. If an enemy were to attack, the lord's army would protect his people. The lord did not provide these important services without getting a lot from the serfs in return. The serfs had to spend most of their time working in the fields, producing food for the lord of the manor and his household. During certain times of the year, such as the planting and the harvesting seasons, the amount of work required would be increased.

Serfs also had to give part of everything they grew or produced to the lord of the manor. They had to give the lord a portion of the milk they got from their goats and cows. They gave him some of the eggs they got from their chickens. They gave him some of the firewood they collected in the forest. And if they used the lord's

Usually a manor estate had a mill.

mill to grind their grain into flour, they had to give the lord some of that, too.

In addition, the serfs had to provide other services to the lord. For example, the serfs had to keep the walls of the lord's manor repaired. If heavy barrels needed to be stacked or moved, the serfs had to do it. If war broke out, serfs had to help defend the lord's land. If the lord had guests, serfs might have to work in the stables taking care of the extra horses, or in the kitchen helping to prepare the food. This meant that the serfs had little time to do chores for themselves.

You might wonder why serfs would agree to give the lord so much. The answer is that within this system there was little choice. The lords had all the power. They had land, weapons, and authority. During periods of unrest, no peasant family could survive without a lord's protection. The Church also supported the feudal system. However, it is also probably true to say that for most ordinary people, so long as they had a home, a job, food to eat, and their lord's protection, they accepted the system they were born into.

The Three-Field System

Despite all this hard work, there was not always enough food for all the people who worked on the land. For example, the soil in England and northern Europe was rich, but the growing season was short and rainy. People had to make the most of what they had. When crops failed, people starved.

In the Middle Ages, people did not have an understanding of science in the way we do today, but they did know quite a lot about farming. People knew that if a field was farmed year after year, it lost its ability to grow healthy crops. They came up with a solution to that problem: the three-field system. In this system, all the cropland on an estate was divided into three fields. Each year, one field was planted in the spring, one field was planted in the fall, and one field was left fallow, or unplanted. The next year, each field would be used differently. One year it might be used to grow crops planted in the spring, like wheat and rye. The next year, it would be used to grow crops planted in the fall, like oats, barley, and beans. The third year the field would be left unplanted. This gave the soil a chance to recover.

Children learned important skills so that they could continue to live and work on the estate.

The three-field system allowed the soil to keep renewing itself. The crops that were planted in the spring used different **nutrients** than those that were planted in the fall. The fields that were not planted had a chance to recover nutrients as old matter broke down and replenished the soil.

Cooperation was the Key

People on a manor estate lived closely together. They had to cooperate with one another. They had to share pastureland. They had to agree on when to plant wheat and oats and when to leave

fields fallow. People had to work together to create or produce goods for trade.

Cooperation was essential to survival. It wasn't really a choice. A smart lord took good care of his serfs. Yet the lord was always the boss. In the society of the Middle Ages, he was superior to the serfs—and few questioned that.

The residents of the manor came together for special holidays. Christmas and Easter and many other religious holidays were celebrated together. The lord, his family, and the serfs would attend church together. There would be a feast, games, and celebrations. In this way, serfs and their lord formed a community that endured through the Middle Ages.

Chapter 8
Life in a Castle

Castles: Dream and Reality You've probably heard fairy tales about kings and queens and castles. There's always something magical going on in the fairy tales. Wizards, witches, and fairy godmothers are likely to be hanging around the castle casting and breaking spells.

The Big Question
....
Why were castles important in the Middle Ages?

Gatehouse

Outer Wall

Drawbridge

Kitchen

Lord's Chamber

Tower

Keep

Great Hall

Moat

A castle in the Middle Ages was like a small city.

Castles are real, however, even if some of the characters in these stories are not. Even today you can see medieval castles all over Europe. In this chapter you'll learn why people built castles and what it was like to live in one.

> **Vocabulary**
>
> **fortress,** n. a fort; a place that has been built to be strong enough to provide protection

Castle Fortress

Castles were designed to be **fortresses**. Kings and some nobles built castles to defend themselves and their estates against attacks. The forts were usually built on high ground. This way the defenders could look down on the attacking enemy. In the early Middle Ages, people built wooden forts, with wooden fences around them. Surrounding the fence was a big ditch, called a moat, that was often filled with water.

If you were attacking such a fort, what would you do? If you answered, "Burn it!", you would have made a good general in the Middle Ages. Wooden castles were easy to build, but they provided little protection against flaming arrows.

Kings and nobles realized that they needed to build castles out of stone to get any real protection from invaders. It was certainly a lot more work. But, by the year 1000, many stone castles were being built in different parts of Europe.

What did a stone castle look like? What was it like to live and fight in one? Read on and find out.

Castle Construction

Put yourself in the place of a king or noble in the Middle Ages. You need to build a castle. What's the first thing you're going to think about? If you answered "location," you get an 'A' for good planning.

A castle needed to be in a place that would be possible to defend. Have you ever wondered why many castles were built on hilltops? A hilltop was easier to defend. Soldiers could see their enemies coming. Castles had high watchtowers for spotting approaching enemies. The enemies had to march up the hill, while soldiers in the castle used weapons against them from above.

Most castles were surrounded by tall stone walls and a water-filled moat. Some castles had more than one moat and more than one wall. Drawbridges could be lowered or raised to create or remove a roadway over the moat. These extra walls and moats provided additional lines of defense. Some castles also had underground tunnels for moving soldiers between different parts of the castle. On top of the walls there were usually walkways from which soldiers could shoot arrows or dump boulders and hot oil down on the attacking enemy.

Keep

Within the castle walls was a central tower called a keep. Some of the area near a castle's keep was open courtyard; other areas were covered. The keep was built to help people hold out for a long time against an enemy who surrounded the castle. In or near the keep were stables, workshops, a large oven, and a kitchen.

There was a **well** for water and stalls for farm animals. There were also storerooms where grains and other foods were kept. These stores were not unlimited, however. Many people—kings, nobles, servants, and soldiers—lived inside a castle. Unless food and supplies were replaced, they would eventually be used up. The chickens would stop laying eggs, and the cows would stop giving milk. Still, people could survive behind a castle's walls for many months.

> **Vocabulary**
> ....
> **well,** n. a hole dug deep into the ground to get water

Castles in War

Castles were strong forts, but well-armed, patient attackers could take a castle.

The battering ram was one method used by attackers. Many soldiers were required to hold up a huge log that was banged against the heavy, ironclad castle doors until the doors broke open. Battering down the door was difficult. Castle doors were strong. And the men holding up the battering ram were under constant attack from defending soldiers high on the castle walls.

Attackers also shot flaming arrows into the keep. The walls may have been stone, but castles still had buildings within made out of wood. They also had hay in the stables, and other items that could catch fire.

Sometimes attackers would dig tunnels under the stone walls and weaken them to the point of collapse.

Nevertheless, since castles were so strong, direct attack rarely worked. Most attackers relied on **siege**, or blockade, to win. In a siege, an attacking army would surround the castle so that food, weapons, and other supplies could not reach the people inside. Castles were prepared for sieges. But after weeks their supplies would run out. Then the attackers would attempt to take over the castle.

Attackers used siege towers, tall wooden towers that rolled on wheels and could hold soldiers. These towers were rolled up to the castle walls. Soldiers climbed up the towers and over the castle walls.

Nevertheless, a castle was a strong fortress. A small army inside could hold out for quite a while against a much larger attacking force.

Sometimes, what decided the battle was action outside the castle. A king or noble under siege would try to get word to other vassals to come to his aid. An army surrounding the castle had to be prepared to fight both the castle troops and another army.

Soldiers tried to get over the castle walls.

Life in a Castle

Castles were very expensive to build, but that doesn't mean that they were very comfortable to live in. In fact, by today's standards, living in an early castle would have been awful. These castles were cold, drafty, and even smelly places.

Many people lived in a castle, but few of them had their own rooms or apartments. Most people lived and ate in the Great Hall, the largest room in the castle. In early castles the king, or noble, and his family might have had beds in the corner of the hall. Everyone else slept on the floor, often piling any clothes they happened to have under and over themselves for warmth.

The Great Hall was also used for meals. Again, only very important people would probably have had chairs to sit in, and everyone else would have sat on long benches alongside tables. After everyone had eaten, the tables were put aside to provide room to sleep. Some early halls did not even have fireplaces. An open fire was built in a stone hearth in the center of the room. It was probably more like camping than luxury living.

It was hard to keep these castles clean. Dogs were allowed to run free in the Great Hall. There were no flush toilets, just closets built

A rich king or noble might hire a jester, also called a fool, to entertain his guests by telling funny stories.

into the edges of walls. Waste fell into pits or moats along the outside of the castle. The most privileged occasionally took baths and washed their hands, but servants did not have many chances to wash.

Over time, castles did become more comfortable, especially for the kings and nobles who lived in them. Fireplaces were added. More people had beds and their own bedrooms. Cold stone walls were hung with **tapestries** or even paneled with wood to cut down on drafts.

The Great Hall was still a center of activity, though. Musical performers, storytellers, and jugglers entertained people while they ate dinner, and long into the evening, too. Various forms of entertainment were especially important during the dark winter nights, when the only source of light and warmth in the castle came from the fire in the Great Hall.

> ### Vocabulary
>
> **tapestry,** n. a handwoven wall hanging that may depict people and / or a scene
>
> **warfare,** n. the activity of fighting a war

Castles were so well constructed that many still stand nearly a thousand years after they were built. Castle building changed, along with advances in weapons and **warfare**, during the Middle Ages. During the early Middle Ages, foot soldiers used bows and arrows as their main weapons. You can see how those thick castle walls would be a good defense against a bow and arrow. But, toward the end of the Middle Ages, the use of cannons in battle made it easier to break down a castle's walls. Can you imagine what it must have been like to be inside a castle that was being hit by cannonballs?

Chapter 9
Days of a Knight

A Knight in Shining Armor Close your eyes. Imagine a line of knights on horseback marching out of a castle across a drawbridge to fight an enemy. It's a bright sunny day, and their armor glints in the sunshine, creating a dazzling sight.

> **The Big Question**
>
> What was the life of a knight like?

> **Vocabulary**
>
> **armor,** n. metal outer covering worn to protect the body in battle

Knights were highly trained soldiers who served a particular noble, or lord, as well as the king. They defended land, castles, and people. Knights rode on horses and were usually in positions of leadership on the battlefield. In military terms, a group of knights could change the outcome of a battle. Many brave and successful knights gained land and power. Over time, stories about knights, good and bad, became the subject of many songs of the Middle Ages.

Knights defended castles in the Middle Ages.

How did a boy become a knight? What was a knight's training like? What did knights do when they weren't fighting battles? Read on to find out.

Pages and Squires

Most knights were the sons of noblemen. They began training to become knights when they were even younger than you are now. When a lord's son was seven or eight years old, he was sent away from his home in a castle or manor to live with a relative or overlord—the person who had granted his father a fief.

Why was he sent away? In his new home he would learn to become a knight. The training took many years. In the first stage of training, the young boy served as a pageboy. A pageboy had to wait on tables and learn the proper manners of a nobleman. Horse-riding skills were also very important. Pages practiced their riding skills all the time. Pages also had to become skilled with a sword, as well as other weapons. At first they learned to fight with fake swords.

Pageboys waited on tables.

When a page was about twelve, he would become a squire. A squire was a personal servant to a particular knight. He went everywhere with the knight. He cleaned the knight's armor and weapons, and cared for his horse. One of his most important jobs was to help the knight get into his heavy armor.

Becoming a Knight

Depending on his rank, the squire might be knighted anytime between the ages of sixteen and twenty. Sometimes a young man who was a member of the highest level of the nobility was knighted at an earlier age. Normally, a young man was knighted in a solemn ceremony. He stayed up all night, praying that he would be a worthy knight. Then he would be presented with spurs, a sword, a shield, and a helmet. His sponsor, usually the lord who had taken him in as a page, would tap him lightly on the shoulder with a sword and dub him Sir Something-or-Other.

Not all knights were born into noble families. The rank of a knight was one of the few positions of nobility that a commoner could hope to attain. Since nobles were usually desperate for brave fighting men, a soldier who showed bravery in battle would occasionally be knighted as a reward.

Life of a Knight

An armored knight on horseback was a great fighting machine. Arrows from enemy archers could bounce off the steel plates. The armor also protected him from an enemy's sword and **lance**.

> **Vocabulary**
>
> **lance,** n. a long weapon with a pointed metal tip, used by horsemen when charging an opponent

In the early Middle Ages, armor was made of sheets of chain mail— metal rings— reinforced with plates of steel in key areas. A shirt of chain mail weighed about twenty-five pounds. Under the mail, the knight wore a shell of thick, hard leather.

Early knights wore chain mail.

By 1400, chain mail was replaced by hinged and fitted steel plates that covered a knight from head to foot. A suit of armor could weigh as much as sixty-five pounds. It was not easy to move around in these metal suits. That's why knights needed squires to help prepare them for battle. However, once on horseback, a knight was a dangerous soldier.

Tournaments and Chivalry

Knights had to stay in shape to face the challenges of battle. During peacetime, knights held **tournaments**.

A tournament was a festive time for everyone on the lord's manor estate. Colorful banners would blow in the breeze on the tournament grounds. Knights painted colorful designs on shields and banners to identify themselves and their families. A tournament would often attract knights and guests from surrounding castles. Lords and ladies wore their finest robes

> **Vocabulary**
>
> **tournament,** n. a series of contests among more than two competitors competing for an overall prize

Tournaments were staged battles where knights could show how skilled they were at jousting.

as they watched their favorite knights charge toward each other on horseback. The goal of the competition was to use a lance to knock the opposing knight off his horse. This was called **jousting**. Nobles and serfs alike would bet money on their favorite knight to win the competition.

Men of Honor

From time to time, knights became a problem for their lords. After all, they were armed men who were trained to settle arguments violently with their swords. Even though they were the lord's vassals, and their job was to protect the lord from enemies, there were times when the lords felt threatened by their own knights.

To control the knights and their potentially dangerous behavior, lords created a set of rules that knights should follow. These rules were called the **Code of Chivalry**. Knights were supposed to be generous, courteous, loyal, and honorable.

> **Vocabulary**
>
> **jousting,** n. a tournament in which two opponents on horseback fight with lances
>
> **"Code of Chivalry,"** (phrase) a set of rules of behavior for knights

The Code of Chivalry required knights to follow certain rules of fighting. For instance, if a knight surrendered, he couldn't try to escape. He had to fight fairly. He could not cheat.

Chivalry also required knights to be kind and thoughtful to women. A part of the code called for knights to show loyalty to the lady they served. Sometimes a knight who fought in a tournament would tie his lady's scarf to his helmet to show that he was fighting on her behalf.

People loved to hear romantic stories about the adventures of knights and their ladies. **Troubadours**, or minstrels, wrote long songs about knights and ladies. Minstrels traveled about, singing and performing these songs for those who would pay to listen.

Mounted Soldiers

What happened to knights? Medieval knights, as we think of them, slowly disappeared, but mounted soldiers did not. Mounted soldiers were still needed in battle. They could lead a charge, or launch a surprise attack. Their horse-riding skills and ability to use a range of weapons meant that they were essential on the battlefield. In the end, mounted soldiers, although no longer noble knights bound to a Code of Chivalry, remained a key part of warfare for hundreds of years more.

Chapter 10
A Serf and His Turf

The Medieval Majority Most people in medieval Europe were not lords, ladies, or knights. They were **peasants**, or common people. Most peasants were serfs who lived on the manor estates and worked for a lord. Some peasants, though, chose to work freely and not serve a lord.

The Big Question

Why does the author say that serfs lived close to the land?

Vocabulary

peasant, n. a person of low social rank, usually a farmer or unskilled worker

Serfs were very much a part of a manor estate. In fact, if a manor estate was taken over by a new lord, the serfs had to remain there to serve the new lord. If you're thinking that being a serf sounds something like being an enslaved person, you're right.

Serfs worked the land on a manor estate.

Sadly, the practice of slavery had existed for thousands of years in different parts of the world. However, the idea of serfdom happened slowly, over time, as the culture and development of medieval Europe took shape. There was, as always, a need for large numbers of workers. However, as more and more people became Christian, the Church became opposed to enslaving Christians. As a result, many people who had been enslaved were freed. These men were known as freedmen.

Unfortunately, freedmen were not always able to make much use of their freedom. Since they had been enslaved all their lives, they were generally poor. Even if they could buy land, they probably would not have been able to protect themselves against warring tribes and powerful lords. Therefore, around the 900s, many freedmen began to trade freedom for **security** by placing themselves under the protection of a feudal lord. This is how many freedmen became serfs.

> **Vocabulary**
> ....
> **security,** n. safety, freedom from danger

It's important to note that medieval serfs had some rights that many enslaved people did not. They could not be sold apart from the land. And they had the right to keep what was left over after paying whatever they owed to their lord. In addition, serfs could pass property on to their children.

The Life of a Serf

There weren't many luxuries for serfs in the Middle Ages. Generally, they led a hard life. Lords were supposed to protect their serfs, but if a lord treated a serf unfairly, there was little a serf could do about it. Serfs had to work extremely hard, and they kept only a small amount of what they grew or made.

By around the year 1000, wood was hard to come by in parts of Europe. The house of a serf typically had a simple wood frame, with a mixture of mud and straw spread in between the wooden beams as walls. The roof of the house was made of straw, and the floor was dirt. In wet weather, the floor turned to mud.

Serfs slept on the floor, perhaps with a layer of straw to provide a little bit of cushioning and warmth. They lived with their animals—chickens, sheep, and pigs. There was no fireplace—just a **hearth** in the middle of the floor, with smoke drifting up through a hole in the roof.

Serfs built the few pieces of furniture they possessed, sewed their own clothes, and grew or raised their own food. In fact, serfs made most everything they needed.

Serfs lived close to the land. They spent most of their days working for the lord of the manor: plowing his fields, planting his seeds, harvesting his crops, and stomping grapes to make his wine. Women were often in charge of small **livestock**. They would shear the master's sheep, spin the wool into yarn, and weave it into cloth. Women also had the job of tending the family vegetable garden and caring for the children.

> **Vocabulary**
>
> **hearth,** n. the bottom of a fireplace
>
> **livestock,** n. the animals kept on a farm

While the serfs prepared food and goods for the master, they had very little themselves. They lived mostly on bread, vegetables, and ale or beer. Interestingly, historians have noted that women's diets seemed to improve after about the year 1000. This helped them live longer and have more children, contributing to the population boom of the High Middle Ages.

Serfs lived on a very simple diet that included bread and vegetables.

If serfs got sick, they depended on village **healers**, who used local herbs to treat illnesses. (Lords might have a professional physician, though his cures were probably not any more advanced.) Of course, not all lords were cruel and heartless. Many realized that if their serfs were going to work hard, they had to be reasonably healthy.

Holidays

While all peasants—serfs or freedmen—faced many difficulties, there were still some good times in their hard lives. Just as we enjoy holidays today, people also enjoyed them in the Middle Ages. In fact, the word *holiday* comes from the "holy days" that were part of the calendar in the Middle Ages. Remember, the

The life of a serf wasn't all work; there was time for fun and games on holy days.

Church was a part of everyday life on the manor estate. People celebrated many more holy days than we do today. With Sundays, saints' days, and other holidays, there were about a hundred days each year when people did little work.

On the holy days, the whole manor attended church. But there was usually more to these holy days than worship. The knightly tournaments you read about earlier often took place on holidays. People held parties with music and dancing. They took part in sports such as bowling and wrestling. They watched jugglers and magicians and listened to traveling troubadours and minstrels. These holidays gave people something to look forward to and lightened the load of serfdom.

Chapter 11
City Life

A Serf Goes to the City Now that you've read about the difficulties of a serf's life, you will not be surprised to learn that sometimes serfs ran away from the manor estate. Some set off to live in the city.

The Big Question

How was life in a medieval city different from life on a manor estate?

Imagine a young serf who has spent his entire life in the countryside. He spends his days in the fields, working side by side with other serfs. Then one day this serf—let's call him Peter—is sent to the city to sell some firewood. He must sell the wood and bring the money back. He leaves home with a cart filled with firewood.

Before the trip, Peter had heard many stories about life in the city. But none of the stories prepared him for the reality of the city.

The hustle and bustle around shops added to the excitement of city life.

For a young man who spends his days in open fields, the crowds of people pressing against him are a terrible shock. Peter would never have guessed that the whole world contained this many people.

Peter is astonished by the gangs of children at play, the women carrying baskets of fruit, and the men pushing small herds of sheep before them. And yet none of these people pay any attention to Peter whatsoever!

The city has many churches. But although there are places to pray, there are dangers, too. Everywhere he looks, he sees thieves and beggars.

Even though it is a sunny day, there are times when Peter can't see the sky to tell what time it is. Some of the narrower streets are shadowed by rows of buildings. He listens for the toll of church bells to know the time.

Peter is excited by all the new sights. But he is also horrified by some of the new smells. As a serf, he is used to a certain amount of odors. But the city smells are worse than anything he has smelled before. People dump waste from animals and people into open drains and ditches. Rainy weather has turned the dirt streets to stinky mud tracks. People selling meat and fish throw their unsold, rotting foods into the streets. Dogs and pigs roam around, trying to make a meal of the garbage. The river is filled with all kinds of garbage, too, including dead animals. Nevertheless, Peter is fascinated with the city and city life.

After selling his firewood, Peter begins to make his way home. Peter cannot stop thinking about the sights and sounds of the city. Then, he makes a decision. He will run away to live there. As he continues home, he begins to make a plan. After a few weeks back on the manor estate, Peter escapes to the city.

What is Peter going to do there? He is a farmer. How can he make his living in the city? Peter isn't sure, but he knows that much of the excitement in the streets is due to people selling and buying goods and services. The streets are full of shops. There are tailors, barbers, furriers, grocers, carpenters, cobblers, leather tanners, and bakers. These shops are more like market stalls opening right onto the busy street. In the back of each shop people make the items that will be sold in the shops.

Peter wants to find a way to work in a shop. He goes from place to place, talking with shopkeepers and clerks about how to find a job.

Guilds

In his discussions with shopkeepers and clerks, Peter discovers that each type of business is

Everywhere Peter looked, people were buying and selling all kinds of goods.

organized into a **guild**. For example, there are guilds for shoemakers, carpenters, hat makers, tailors, clock makers, and jewelers. The leading members of each guild, called master craftsmen, make rules for their craft in the city. (They are called craftsmen because they are mostly men, though there are some women, too.) The guilds set standards for things like product quality and training.

Vocabulary

guild, n. a group of businessmen who control a certain craft

apprentice, n. a person who is learning a trade from a master craftsman

Guilds require would-be members to train for a certain number of years with a guild member. Most start out as **apprentices** when they are children, helping their master at work. Peter learns that he is too old to start as an apprentice.

Young children became apprentices. They spent many years learning a craft or skill.

When an apprentice proves himself or herself to be skillful in the craft, he or she is promoted to **journeyman**. At this point he or she is allowed to practice the trade in the community and earn wages. A journeyman might work for the master he apprenticed with. Or he might go into business with another journeyman. A journeyman will work in this way for many years to prove himself to be highly skilled in his craft and a reliable member of the guild. Finally, the journeyman can request that the guild raise him to the status of master. Part of the process of becoming a master require that the journeyman produce a **masterpiece**. A masterpiece is a perfect example of a finished product for his craft. For example, a shoemaker's masterpiece is a pair of perfect shoes. The masterpiece is proof that a journeyman has the skills to continue the high standards of the guild.

> **Vocabulary**
>
> **journeyman,** n. a guild member who is considered qualified to work for wages in a particular trade
>
> **masterpiece,** n. a perfect example of a finished product of some craft

The Growth of Trade and Cities

Between the fall of Rome and about the year 1000, there was not much travel or trade among areas in Europe. As Europe became somewhat safer from bandits and outlaws, trade began to increase. Merchants now needed people to carry their goods to other towns and cities to sell. Peter decides to look for work in the growing trade between cities.

Cities in Europe grew along with trade and business. London, Paris, Venice, and many other cities began to expand. Many people preferred city life to life on a manor estate.

The growth of towns and cities had an impact on local governments, businesses, and the feudal system itself. Eager to establish local governments, towns offered their king, or sometimes a lord, a sum of money for a **charter**. A charter was a document that granted townspeople

permission to elect their own mayors, sheriffs, and other officials. However, the only people who could vote in these elections were the powerful merchants.

Churches, government buildings, guildhalls, shops, and houses crowded behind the safety of city walls during the later Middle Ages.

From around 1000 onward, the feudal lords slowly began to lose influence and power to the kings. People were required to be loyal to the king, but their ties to lords were weakening. Kings used the wealth from towns and cities to become more powerful. Over time, strong kings established kingdoms such as England, France, and Castile (central Spain). However, just as the decline of the Western Roman Empire happened over a long period of time, the decline of the feudal system took many years, too.

Chapter 12
Women in the Middle Ages

How Women Lived So far you have been reading mostly about the lives of men in the Middle Ages. Unfortunately, there is less information about women in Europe during this time. However, there were some women whose lives were so extraordinary that they became famous.

The Big Question

What was it like to be a woman in the Middle Ages?

Most men *and* women of this time were peasants and serfs. Women had the same hard lives as their fathers, husbands, and brothers. Just like boys, girls did farm work when they were young. They had to haul water, tend to crops, and care for animals.

Most women in the Middle Ages had the same hard lives that men had.

Adult women spent much of their time weaving, cooking, feeding farm animals, and caring for children. During really busy times, women and men worked together in the fields. They needed to grow enough food for the lord of the manor, as well as for their own families.

Poor Health

In the Middle Ages, people had very different ideas about health and medicine than we do today. Many people died from diseases, and few lived as long as the average modern American. Nobles and wealthy townspeople were a little healthier than serfs because their diet was better, and they certainly had enough to eat. But, because people at the time had no understanding of germs or viruses, people did not recognize the relationship between good **hygiene** and good health.

As a result, natural occurrences such as giving birth could be dangerous. Women and their babies often died in childbirth. And even if they survived childbirth, many young children died of illness before they reached adulthood. So there was much sadness and tragedy in the lives of women in the Middle Ages.

> **Vocabulary**
>
> **hygiene,** n.
> cleanliness
>
> **religious,** adj.
> relating to beliefs about God or several gods to explain how the world started, why things happen, and how people should live in the world

Convent Leaders

There weren't many career choices for women, either. One possibility was to choose a **religious** life. In the religious world of the Middle Ages, sending a daughter to a convent was thought of as an act of religious **devotion**. Convents were like monasteries, but for women; the members devoted their lives to God. And just as monasteries had a big impact on life in the Middle Ages, so did convents. Women in convents devoted their lives to prayer and to helping people. Even girls who were peasants or serfs could join a convent. However, even in the convent, their lives were different from the girls who came from wealthier families. While everyone prayed together, the poorer girls worked in the kitchens and in the fields. Basically they did the same kinds of jobs their families did outside the convent walls.

The leader of a convent was called an **abbess**. During times of conflict, some leaders of convents were successful negotiators. They arranged peace agreements between warring nobles.

> **Vocabulary**
> ....
> **devotion,** n. strong loyalty to a cause or belief
>
> **abbess,** n. the leader of a convent
>
> **composer,** n. a person who writes music

Hildegard of Bingen

Even though little is known of women generally, the fame of one medieval nun has lasted to this day. As evidence of this, we can listen to modern recordings of the music she wrote in the Middle Ages. She is one of the earliest **composers** in history whose life story is known to us. She wrote a musical drama or play. It is the only one of its kind known from this period.

Hildegard of Bingen was born in 1098 in Germany. She began having religious **visions** when she was a child. She had these visions throughout her life. The visions were powerful and affected her greatly. In one vision, for example, she described how "the heavens were opened and a blinding light of exceptional brilliance flowed through [her] entire brain."

When she was still quite young, her parents sent her to live with a famous holy woman who was to be her teacher. This woman's name was Jutta. Jutta taught Hildegard how to read and write. Hildegard also received her religious education from Jutta. Slowly, people began hearing about Hildegard and her remarkable visions. Her visions inspired her to write beautiful music, poems, plays, and books. Hildegard's works were admired by the pope and by other religious and political leaders. Eventually, Hildegard started a new convent in the German town of Bingen.

Some of Hildegard's visions, such as this one of the tree of life, were described and illustrated in books during her lifetime.

Trade and Learning

Although women had fewer options than men, it was possible for women to go into business with their husbands. And if their husbands died, they were allowed to continue to work. There were some women who managed to start up their own businesses, though this was not typical. Historians have found records of women who worked as brewers, glassmakers, weavers, and in other trades.

One important development during the Middle Ages that sadly did not benefit women was the creation of **universities**. The first ones were started in Italy, England, and France. These universities advanced learning in many areas, but women were not allowed to attend. This made it impossible for women to be officially trained for careers in law or medicine.

Women in convents, though, continued to learn and share knowledge. Certain convents trained women to teach young children, and others trained women to provide health care and help families.

Only men could attend a university, as this image of life at the University of Paris in the Middle Ages reveals.

Chapter 13
William the Conqueror

William of Normandy In the 1000s, in a part of France called Normandy, there lived an eight-year-old boy named William. One day, William was a happy child, the son of a powerful lord, the **duke** of Normandy. The next day, William's father was dead.

The Big Question

How did William's successful invasion of England affect the English language?

Vocabulary

duke, n. a male noble who rules a small territory

Young William was named duke. Now, you might think that being a duke would be fun, but not for William. What it meant for him was that other powerful lords in Europe, men who had been family friends, now wanted to kill him.

William the Conqueror was born at Falaise Castle in Normandy.

What was going on? Why would these friends want William dead? The world of **politics** in the Middle Ages was often a violent place. As his father's oldest son, William was the rightful duke. But that didn't stop others from trying to kill him to become the duke themselves. William survived, thanks to help from the king of France.

Why is this story important? Because William, duke of Normandy, later fought and won one of the most important battles in the Middle Ages, the Battle of Hastings. This battle changed the history of the British Isles and helped create the English language you are reading right now.

> **Vocabulary**
>
> **politics,** n. the activities of a leader or ruler running a government
>
> **"claim to the throne,"** (idiom) the right to be the ruler

The Battle of Hastings

The English Channel is the body of water that flows between England and Europe. Normandy lies along the European side of the English Channel. Today, Normandy is a region of France, but in the 1000s it was a duchy, a territory ruled by a duke. The king of France had little real power there.

In 1066, the king of England died without any children. Several people claimed that they should be the next king of England. One was an English lord named Harold, who had himself crowned king. Another person with a **claim to the throne** was William, duke of Normandy.

In late September 1066, William and his army of knights and foot soldiers crossed the English Channel. King Harold was in the north

The English Channel

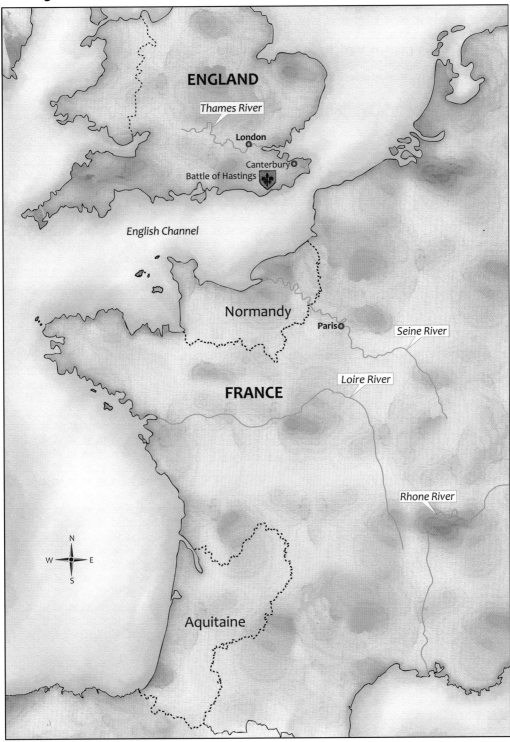

The English Channel separates England and France. To get to England, the Normans had to cross the English Channel.

of England, having just defeated another king who wanted to rule England. He and his army marched south. They met William and the Norman forces on October 14, 1066, near the coastal town of Hastings. The English soldiers were in a line on a hillside. At first, the English soldiers turned back the Norman charge. But when the Normans retreated, the English soldiers broke ranks and chased them. This was just the chance William needed. He turned on the disorganized English army and defeated them. King Harold was killed in the battle.

William marched his army to London, the capital, and was crowned king. William, duke of Normandy, was now King William I of England. He is perhaps better known as William the **Conqueror**.

Vocabulary

conqueror, n. a person who takes control of a territory after an invasion

The English soldiers formed a defensive line.

A New Language

William's conquest of England has had a big impact on our lives, even for those of us who have never even visited England. Before William arrived, most people in England spoke Anglo-Saxon (Old English). This was the language of the Germanic people who had arrived in England after the fall of the Roman Empire.

The Normans spoke an early form of French. At first, the common people of England spoke Anglo-Saxon, and all the nobles (most of whom were the relatives and friends of William the Conqueror) spoke French. Over time, the French and Anglo-Saxon languages blended. That is why English includes a mixture of French and Germanic words. So it is with *cow* and *beef*. When we talk about cows, we are using a Germanic word that the Anglo-Saxon people used before William came to England. When we sit down to eat beef, we are using a French word that was brought to England after William's invasion.

Historical Records

The Middle Ages were a long, long time ago. There are many people and events that we know very little about because there are few surviving **records**. But we know a good

Vocabulary

record, n. evidence of events from the past

It is believed that one of William's brothers ordered the creation of the *Bayeux Tapestry* as a record of the Battle of Hastings. Because of the tapestry, (which is actually an embroidered cloth), we can picture a battle that happened almost a thousand years ago.

deal about England in the time of William the Conqueror because several important historical records have survived. Two of the most significant of these are the *Bayeux* (/bie*yoo/) *Tapestry* and the *Domesday Book*.

Sometimes, when a new ruler takes over, he leaves things pretty much as they were before. Not William! He started to change England from top to bottom. William threw many of the Anglo-Saxon lords off their lands and estates and replaced them with his Norman friends who had fought with him at Hastings.

William wanted to know more about his new country. He ordered that a list be made of all the people and valuable items in the kingdom. The king's agents went all over England, visiting even the smallest villages and most distant settlements. They recorded the names of the lords and their lands. They recorded the number of small landowners, knights, and serfs serving each feudal lord. They counted pigs, sheep, and other livestock and made notes about the forests in each region. If there was a mill or some other business in town, William's agents made a note of it. They even kept a record of how many beehives there were in each region.

The *Domesday Book*

This survey of William's kingdom was called the *Domesday Book*. It took several years and a lot of money to finish. But it was worth the expense, for the book let William know exactly who lived where. It allowed him to keep track of all the rent and **taxes** that were due to him.

But the *Domesday Book* was about more than taxes and money. William made sure that every lord listed in the book swore an oath of loyalty to him as the king of England. Anybody who did not cooperate

with William's agents or refused to swear loyalty to the king was severely punished. The *Domesday Book* is a treasure for historians of the Middle Ages. It gives an accurate picture of a feudal kingdom more than 900 years ago. For example, we know that there were two million people living in England during the reign of William I.

This page from the *Domesday Book* shows the number of oxen, plows, villagers, woodlands, and lands that were counted in a particular place.

How did this book get its name? It is actually an old-fashioned spelling of the word *doomsday*. Some people think it was called that because people who did not cooperate with the king's agents were killed. But this is not the real reason. In fact, it was probably called the *Domesday Book* because doomsday is the biblical day of judgment and accounting. That was exactly what William's agents did when they arrived in a town—they counted up the people and judged how much everyone and everything was worth.

Chapter 14
Henry II

Weak Kings and Trouble in the Land King William died in 1087. Just as he had done, the kings that followed ruled England and parts of France. However, none of these kings were as strong as William the Conqueror, and that caused problems in England.

The Big Question

How did the shield tax benefit King Henry II and future kings?

After King William died, various nobles fought for power.

Over time, various nobles, seeing that William's **successors** were weak, tried to seize power. This led to constant warfare and a general breakdown of law and order. Without a strong king to hold them in line, these power-hungry lords fought each other, and the king.

For ordinary people, these were hard times. Armies robbed people and killed anyone who resisted. Lords needed money to fight their wars, so they increased taxes on their estates. Trade could not be conducted safely, so businesses suffered.

A Strong King Makes Order

Once again, as in 1066, a hero arrived from across the English Channel. Henry II was the great-grandson of William the Conqueror. When Henry was only two, his grandfather, Henry I, died. Because of Henry's young age, the throne was taken by one of his cousins. However, when Henry was twenty-one, he won the support of a number of nobles and was crowned King Henry II in Westminster Abbey, in December of 1154.

Henry II challenged the lords who threatened him.

Bright and well-educated, Henry spoke French and Latin, but he did not speak much English. Usually he was good-natured and gentle, but he was known to have a terrible temper.

A Man of Pleasure

Henry loved to hunt, and he loved to go hawking. Hawking was a sport that used trained falcons and birds of prey to capture other birds. These hunting birds were treated with care, like expensive hunting dogs. Henry loved to travel around with a favorite bird perched on his leather glove. He and his nobles often brought their trained birds to the banquet hall and fed them treats.

The King Is Number One

Henry was full of energy and ideas. He was determined to end the wars that had plagued England. He also intended to make sure the king would always be stronger than the lords who served him. One of his first acts as king was to take to the field of battle and go after lords who had grown greedy and too powerful.

Law and Order

Henry soon realized that he needed more than a good army to be a strong leader. He needed laws and **government** to make sure the kingdom ran in an orderly manner. Henry turned his attention to the way the laws and courts worked in England.

> **Vocabulary**
>
> **government**, n.
> a small group of people who have the authority to make rules for a much larger group, such as people living in a particular city, region, or country

Royally appointed judges traveled to hear cases.

The **court** system was very confusing. Lords were in charge of the courts for certain types of crimes in certain places. The king was in charge of other courts, and the Church was in charge of still others.

There were also different types of **trials**. In some trials, people accused of crimes might be forced to "prove" their innocence through combat; or they might be forced to pick up a red-hot piece of iron with a bare hand. If the hand didn't heal quickly, the person was considered guilty.

What a mess! Henry II set up a group of **administrators** who could run the legal system. He held several conferences with nobles and Church leaders. In these meetings, Henry ordered a fairer legal system and the right to trial by **jury**. The job of people on a jury is to first hear evidence and then decide whether they think the accused person is guilty or innocent. The jury system Henry began is still in use today.

Other Improvements

Henry made many other changes in his effort to make the king more powerful. Remember how vassals owed their lord military service? Henry felt there were too many times when this arrangement didn't work. Lords who were not fully behind the king did not always support him. They often sent fewer soldiers than he needed. Sometimes they completely ignored the king's request for military aid.

Henry decided to change the law. He introduced the shield tax. The shield tax required lords to send money instead of soldiers. Henry could then use the money to hire his own soldiers. His own soldiers would be ready to fight and would be loyal to him. Henry also started a program of rebuilding stone castles.

A Long Line of Kings

Henry and the kings who came after him were known as the Plantagenet (/plan*taj* ə*nit/) **dynasty**, or rulers belonging to the same family. The name *Plantagenet* probably came from a yellow flower called *Planta genista* that Henry's father liked to wear as a sort of badge or emblem. Henry II was the first Plantagenet king of England.

Chapter 15
Thomas Becket

A Hard-Working Man Henry II depended on a group of trusted advisors to help him run his large kingdom. The one he relied on most of all was named Thomas Becket.

The Big Question

Why did Henry II regret the words he spoke about Thomas Becket?

Becket was not born into a noble household. He was the son of a merchant. Becket became a priest, and through hard work and intelligence he began to rise through the ranks of the Church. At the same time, he also began to work his way up in the world of politics.

In 1154, one of the first acts of the newly crowned King Henry II was to appoint Thomas Becket to the job of chancellor. The chancellor was the king's highest advisor.

King Henry II relied on the advice of Thomas Becket.

This was an important job. Becket worked hard, but he also enjoyed his hard-earned position. His household soon became as grand as any in the kingdom. In fact, Becket's house in London became known as the place to be. King Henry didn't care much for hosting fancy feasts. But everyone, including the king and queen, went to Becket's for a good time. He had a grand banquet hall. In those days, people thought that eating raw fruit was unhealthy and that vegetables were for the poor. So, for the rich, meals consisted of meat, poultry, and bread.

These nobles didn't just dine on chicken and roast beef: the plates in Becket's household carried cooked starlings, seagulls, herons, and storks. Peacocks were roasted and presented *with* their spectacular tail feathers. A roasted swan was arranged on a bed of green pastry so it looked as if the bird were gliding over a pond.

Thomas Becket knew how to entertain. But in his personal life, he remained a serious, **devout** priest. He also worked hard at his job, helping King Henry bring order to the kingdom.

> **Vocabulary**
>
> **devout,** adj.
> showing deep religious feelings

Archbishop of Canterbury

Working closely together, Becket and Henry became good friends. Becket was fifteen years older than Henry, but they got along well. Becket gave the young king lots of advice. He helped Henry run his kingdom well. You already know that Henry was trying to solve certain problems that existed within the legal system of England. This included getting rid of the **loopholes** in the Church courts. When the man who

Vocabulary

loophole, n. a way around a law or rule

was the archbishop of Canterbury died, Henry suggested to the pope that his good friend Thomas Becket should become the next archbishop of Canterbury.

Being the archbishop of Canterbury was a great honor and a big promotion. There was only one problem: Becket didn't want the job. It may have been a great honor, but Becket saw the trouble that would lie ahead.

Since the king and the Church were often in conflict, he knew that Church officials would see him as being on the king's side, instead of theirs. He also knew that if he were going to do his job well, there would be times when he would have to disagree with the king.

But when a king asks you to do something, it's difficult to say no. Becket became archbishop of Canterbury. At first, he and King Henry got along despite some minor conflicts about the Church courts. However, to everyone's surprise, Becket took his new job *very* seriously. Most people did not know about the serious side of Thomas Becket. Now they saw who he really was. The big parties and banquets came to an end. Becket put aside his fancy robes and furs and wore simple clothes and coarsely woven shirts. He spent a lot of time praying, meditating, and studying the Bible.

Thomas Becket took his role as archbishop of Canterbury very seriously.

Trouble and Tragedy

King Henry was surprised by the change in his friend's behavior. But he grew truly alarmed when Becket opposed him on questions about the role of the Church in the legal system.

King Henry proposed a new law that took a great deal of power away from the Church courts and gave it to the king. Henry let Becket know that he expected him to support the new law. Instead, the archbishop opposed the king.

Hot-tempered King Henry was enraged at the actions of his former friend. This was the beginning of a **feud** that, thanks to Henry's bad temper, kept getting worse.

> **Vocabulary**
>
> **feud**, n. a long and bitter argument

Henry charged Becket with disobeying the law. He took some of Becket's lands away. Becket felt so threatened that he left England secretly and spent a few years living outside the country. Twice they tried to end their conflict, but again and again they quarreled. Eventually, the pope ordered the king to end his quarrel with the archbishop or face **excommunication**. Henry gave in because he could not risk the anger of the pope.

Becket Returns

Eventually Becket felt it was safe to return to England. The feuding was not over, though. Shortly after he returned to England, Becket excommunicated some powerful nobles who were friends of the king.

Henry was furious. One night in December of 1170, Henry was at a castle in Normandy. In a fit of anger, he cried out, "Will no one rid me of this upstart priest?" No one really knows what Henry meant by these words. Were his words simply an expression of anger, or did Henry *really* want to be rid of Becket?

It so happened that four young knights, hotheaded and eager for the king's favor, heard the king speak. They took his words as a serious call for action.

Slipping out of the castle that night, the knights found a boat to take them across the English Channel. At the cathedral in Canterbury, they found Becket conducting a religious service. The

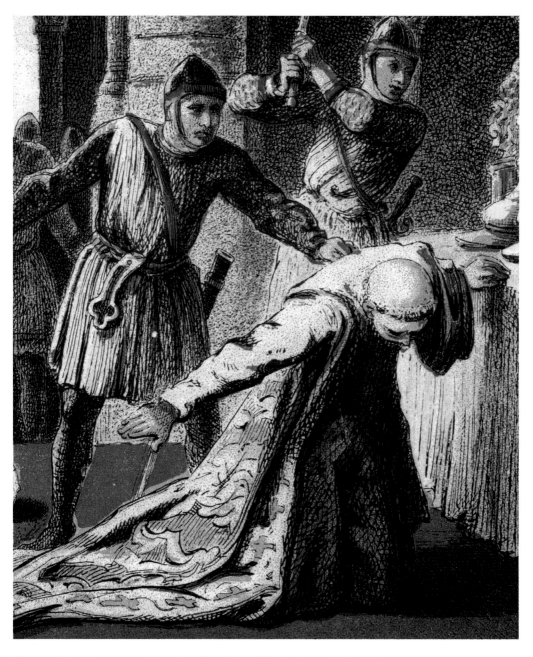

Thomas Becket was murdered on the altar of Canterbury Cathedral.

heavily armed knights expected Becket to be afraid and to beg
for his life. Becket did not run. He only began to struggle when
the four men tried to drag him out of the cathedral. He declared
himself "ready to die for my Lord," and then the knights killed him,
right there in the cathedral.

Reaction

The murder shocked all of Europe, but few were more upset by the crime than Henry himself. Just as Becket himself had done on becoming archbishop, Henry removed his fine clothing and dressed in sackcloth, an uncomfortable cloth made of coarse fibers. He poured ashes over his head. Like dressing in sackcloth, this was a way to show sorrow. He refused to eat or sleep.

Finally he made a **pilgrimage** to Canterbury. When he was three miles from the cathedral, he got off his horse and removed his shoes. The king walked the last three miles barefoot. By the time he arrived, "his footsteps . . . seemed to be covered in blood . . . for his tender feet being cut by the hard stones, a great quantity of blood flowed from them on to the ground."

> **Vocabulary**
>
> **pilgrimage,** n. a journey undertaken for a religious purpose
>
> **shrine,** n. a place considered holy because it is associated with a religious person or saint

Three years after his murder, Becket was made a saint by the Church. His tomb in Canterbury Cathedral became the most popular **shrine** in England. Henry was rid of his "upstart priest," but he had also lost one of his closest friends. Yet Henry would find even more trouble before his rule finally ended. This time, the source would be someone who was even closer to him than his old friend Thomas Becket.

Chapter 16
Eleanor of Aquitaine

Queen of France Eleanor of Aquitaine (/ak*wit*aen/) was an extraordinary woman, especially in an age when women had very little power. She was beautiful, charming, and intelligent, and came from a powerful family. She could read and write (unusual for a woman in the 1100s), play the harp, and ride a horse as well as any man.

The Big Question

Why do you think the author describes Eleanor as extraordinary?

But the most important thing that Eleanor had was land. She was the **duchess** of Aquitaine, one of the largest and richest regions of what is now France. Aquitaine was a region rich in rivers (its name came from the Roman word for "land of waters"), olive groves, vineyards, wheat fields, orchards, and forests.

Vocabulary

duchess, n. a female noble who is the wife or widow of a duke or who rules a small territory herself

Eleanor of Aquitaine married Louis, the son of the king of France, when she was fifteen.

As duchess, she was a vassal of the king of France, but she controlled more land than he did.

Still, she had to do what the king said. So when the king told the fifteen-year-old Eleanor that she was going to marry Louis, his sixteen-year-old son, whom she had never met, she didn't question it. Eleanor had always known that she would marry a young nobleman some day and that her marriage would be based on land rather than love. Shortly after her marriage, the old king died, and Louis became king of France. Eleanor became the queen.

At first, the two teenagers got along quite well, but disappointment followed. Eleanor gave birth to two girls instead of the son the king needed to follow him on the throne. Eleanor hated the royal castle in Paris. It was cold and dreary. She missed sunny Aquitaine. Louis was not as bold and dashing as Eleanor's father and grandfather had been. To make things worse, Louis got more and more interested in religion. Was she looking around for a new husband? No one really knows for sure, but one day a young nobleman named Henry came to Paris.

The End of a Royal Marriage

You've met Henry before. The young man Eleanor met was the same handsome, energetic, and charming man who later became Henry II. When Eleanor first met him, he wasn't yet king of England. He was Henry of Anjou (/on*joo/), and he controlled the lands north of Aquitaine. Eleanor's husband, the king of France, saw Henry as his chief rival for power. Little did he know how much of a rival Henry would become.

Shortly after she met Henry, Eleanor asked for an **annulment**, or a cancellation of her marriage to Louis. Although King Louis was sad that she wanted to end the marriage, their failure to produce a son was a serious issue. The religious king wondered whether the failure was a sign of God's displeasure, as Eleanor claimed. After fifteen years of marriage, the marriage was annulled, and Louis and Eleanor went their separate ways.

Eleanor returned to Aquitaine. Even if she had wanted to remain unmarried for a while, Eleanor soon saw that it was impossible. Eleanor needed the protection of a husband.

> ### Vocabulary
> **annul,** v. to cancel; to make no longer legal or true
>
> **proposal,** n. an offer of marriage

Queen of England

No one knows for sure when or how Henry and Eleanor agreed to marry or who made the first **proposal**. Yet, two months after the annulment of her marriage to Louis, Eleanor and Henry were married.

These two were far better suited to each other than Eleanor and Louis had been. Henry and Eleanor were both intelligent, bold, and spirited people who admired learning, literature, and power. In the first thirteen years of their marriage, Henry and Eleanor had eight children, including five sons.

Together, they were the most powerful couple in Europe. Their lands and wealth ensured the support of powerful nobles. Henry had the knights, ships, and power he needed to sail across the Channel and claim the throne of England.

For fourteen years, Henry and Eleanor ruled together over their kingdom, which stretched from Scotland to Spain. Look at the map to see what lands they controlled.

Sadly, this marriage began to fail, too. Eleanor returned to Aquitaine with her children. It wasn't long before some of her sons were teenagers. The young sons were impatient for power of their own. Henry gave them titles but no power. Eleanor encouraged her sons to think about the day when they could oppose their father.

France and England in the 1100s

Henry and Eleanor ruled a vast area.

Meanwhile, Eleanor **held court** in Aquitaine. She hired the best poets and troubadours to entertain her and her children. She favored stories of courtly love in which brave young knights performed feats of courage for their ladies. She encouraged her sons to be brave and

dashing. She also encouraged interesting and witty conversation. Her court was considered to be the most civilized place in Europe.

Royal Rivals

The murder of Thomas Becket was a turning point in Henry II's rule over England. Many powerful nobles in England blamed Henry for Becket's murder. Eleanor saw an opportunity and encouraged her sons to take advantage of the king's new weakness by rebelling against him. With their mother's help, the sons were able to get the support of several powerful nobles. Remember, it was King Henry who had just recently stripped them of their power.

The sons, with the help of certain nobles, did lead a rebellion against their father. But Henry was still a masterful warrior. Henry put down the rebellion and placed Eleanor under house arrest, making her a prisoner in one of his castles. There she stayed until his death some fifteen years later.

King Richard I

When Henry died, their eldest son, Richard, became king. Richard immediately had his mother freed. The new king was very close to his mother. Eleanor saw many of the same qualities in Richard that she had first admired in Henry. He was dashing, handsome, adventurous, and energetic. Richard would have been a great king, except for one

Richard I led thousands of soldiers in what is known as the Third Crusade. The crusades were attempts by Europeans to reclaim the Holy Land from Muslim control.

problem: he did not have his father's gift for governing.

During his ten years as king, Richard the Lionhearted, as he was called, hardly set foot in England. He was too busy leading **crusades** overseas. At one point he was taken prisoner and held for **ransom**. Eleanor raised the money to get him released.

The Crusades

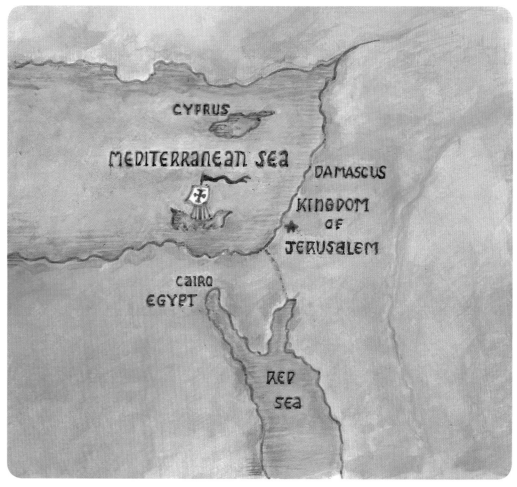

Crusaders traveled to the Middle East and to North Africa. These wars began in 638 when Arab armies captured Jerusalem.

If the king was away so much, who ruled England while he was gone? His younger brother, John, and his mother, Queen Eleanor, that's who! John was not as popular as Richard, but his mother was. Just as her husband Henry II had done, she worked on solving problems in England. She introduced standard coins, and a system of weights and measures, making it easier to conduct business. She also did away with a number of unfair laws. These **reforms** made her popular with her subjects.

When Richard was killed during one of his adventures, Eleanor was heartbroken. John became king of England. By this time Eleanor was nearly eighty. She retired to a convent, where she died at the age of eighty-two.

The statue of Queen Eleanor on her tomb shows her holding a book. This emphasizes just how unusual a woman she was for her time.

Chapter 17
Magna Carta

The Landless Son The youngest child of Eleanor of Aquitaine and Henry II was a boy named John. Although John would become Henry's favorite son, Henry had already given his most valuable fiefs to his other sons.

The Big Question

Why is Magna Carta so important?

As a young man, John was given the nickname "John Lackland" because he did not have any land of his own. No one expected John to become king because he had so many older brothers. The throne of England was usually given to the oldest living son. In fact, when John was very young, he was sent to be raised in a monastery. Like Hildegard of Bingen, he was supposed to dedicate his life to God. All of that changed, however.

Except for Richard, all of John's older brothers died before reaching the throne. When Richard died, the thirty-two-year-old John was the sole surviving son of Henry II, so he became king of England.

No one expected John to become king.

For hundreds of years, historians considered John to be one of the worst kings in English history. Today, many historians say that he wasn't such a terrible king after all. John did make mistakes, though. Like other Plantagenet kings, he was intelligent and hardworking, with a strong sense of justice. But people did not trust him, and intelligence and hard work were not enough to win wars.

A Series of Defeats

Five years after John took the throne, the king of France attacked Normandy and Anjou. These were the lands that John's father, Henry II, had brought to his marriage with Eleanor. John was unable to defend these lands.

If it wasn't bad enough that John lost important lands to the French king, now he had to ask his nobles to pay higher taxes to cover the costs of the war. If nobles refused to pay, or could not pay, King John took **hostages**. In other words, he might hold a relative or important servant prisoner until someone paid up. John also demanded taxes from people who lived in cities, especially wealthy merchants. This put the merchants on the same side as the angry nobles.

John seemed to have a special talent for making enemies. **Barons**, a type of English noble, and powerful townspeople were already angry with him. Then John disagreed with the pope. King John did not like the

> ### Vocabulary
>
> **hostage**, n. a person taken by force and held prisoner, then often later exchanged for money or other demands
>
> **baron**, n. a lord; a lower rank in the British nobility

man the pope had chosen to become archbishop of Canterbury. Pope Innocent III was probably the most powerful man in Europe at this time. It was not a good idea to disagree with him. The pope decided to challenge John.

King John

When John seized property that belonged to the Church, the pope responded by sending out an order to close the churches in England. With the churches closed, priests could not perform many of their duties. People could not receive a Christian burial. The pope wanted the king's subjects to believe that it was all King John's fault. Then the pope excommunicated the king. John had no choice but to give in. He agreed to recognize the pope's choice for archbishop.

A Great Charter

This was not enough to satisfy the demands of the angry barons and townspeople. In 1215, they prepared a list of demands known as Magna Carta, which is Latin for "Great Charter." It laid out rules for what the king could and could not do to nobles, freemen, and the Church. The barons said they would go to war against John if he did not accept the document. When he saw he could not defeat the barons, John agreed to meet their demands.

At a meeting in a meadow outside London, John placed his seal of approval on the document. Copies of Magna Carta were made by hand and carried all over the kingdom. John died the next year of a fever as a new war raged through his kingdom. Over the next eleven years, Magna Carta was revised several times. The final **version** was approved in 1225 by John's son, Henry III. In 1297, it officially became part of English law.

> **Vocabulary**
>
> **version**, n. a draft; a form of something, like a document, that is different from other forms of the same thing

This is a page from the final version of Magna Carta approved in 1225 by John's son, Henry III.

Why is Magna Carta important? It is an important document in the history of the rule of law. In Magna Carta, a king agreed that he had to rule according to laws. Many of Magna Carta's rules or laws lasted through the years that followed. A few ideas in the United States Constitution can be traced directly to Magna Carta. Modern **democracy**, with its emphasis on freedoms and **rights**, was still a long way in the future. But one of the first steps was taken when a group of barons forced King John to accept Magna Carta in a meadow outside the city of London.

> ## Vocabulary
>
> **democracy**, n. a form of government in which people choose their leaders; a country with this form of government
>
> **right**, n. a legal promise

Chapter 18
A New Kind of Government

England's First Parliament King John died the year after he accepted Magna Carta. When he died, his son Henry III was only nine years old. So England was ruled by a **council** of barons until Henry was old enough to rule.

The Big Question

What is the difference between a system of government with representatives and one with a monarch?

During these years of rule by the council, barons often settled their disputes in discussions rather than by going to war. Instead of hard times, England enjoyed a period of peace.

Henry's grandfather, Henry II, had created a system of government that worked well. For hundreds of years, England had been divided into counties. Under Henry II's system of government, each county had a sheriff who managed local affairs. The whole country was divided into six **circuits**, or districts. Each circuit had three judges. All the judges enforced the same laws, which made governing the country easier.

Vocabulary

council, n. a group of people organized to govern

circuit, n. an area or district through which a judge travels to hold court sessions

Simon de Montfort led a revolt against the king.

But once Henry III was old enough to rule, there were problems. Henry did not like to make decisions, and he began to challenge existing laws. He also gave many jobs in the government to his wife's friends and relatives. Once again the barons rebelled, as they had against Henry's father, King John. They demanded that the king allow a council of barons to rule. At first, Henry agreed. Then he changed his mind, and war broke out between the king and some of the barons.

A New Idea

Eventually King Henry III was captured by Simon de Montfort, the leader of the barons' revolt. But what were they to do with the rebellious king? Simon de Montfort decided to try something new. He called a meeting of landowning nobles, leaders of the Church, knights, and **citizens** from the towns. He wanted to find another way to pass laws and run the country. Since it was not practical for *everyone* to come to this meeting, Montfort had each group vote for representatives who would go instead.

This historic meeting was the first time that **representatives** from all classes, except serfs, met together to make decisions. This was the beginning of England's parliamentary system. More than one hundred people met for two months. Although not democratic by modern standards, it was a new idea. This first

> **Vocabulary**
>
> **citizen**, n. in the Middle Ages, a skilled tradesman, artisan, or important merchant who was a resident of a city
>
> **representative**, n. a person in government who makes decisions and votes on behalf of a group of people

Parliament was an exciting but short-lived affair. King Henry escaped from capture. His army defeated the rebels and killed Simon de Montfort. Parliament was disbanded.

> **Vocabulary**
>
> **parliament**, n. a group made up of representatives and the monarch, who make the laws for a country; a term used especially in England to describe the lawmaking part of the government

The Model Parliament

The next king, Edward I, learned from the mistakes of his father, Henry III, and his grandfather, John. Edward needed a lot of money. He was fighting a war, he was building expensive castles in Wales, and he was also trying to conquer Scotland. Instead of ordering people to pay taxes, Edward decided to try something different. He used some of Simon de Montfort's ideas. He called together representatives from throughout his kingdom. He hoped to win their cooperation in raising money for his projects.

In 1295, what became known as the Model Parliament met in Westminster, now part of London. It included two knights from each county and two citizens from each city and town. These representatives were elected, not appointed. Also attending were priests, various nobles, and bishops. It has become known as the Model Parliament because every parliament in England since then has been based on this one.

Edward was a wise king. He realized that he would be more likely to get the money he needed and to avoid bad feelings if he worked with the representatives in Parliament. His plan worked. Parliament agreed to give the king the money he needed. But Edward had set in motion a big change. Many people now thought that the king must always ask Parliament for money. Also, they argued that he couldn't impose taxes without first getting the approval of Parliament. This was not at all what Edward had intended. Once again, the king and Parliament disagreed.

King Edward I, surrounded by a king of Scotland, a prince of Wales, Church leaders, and representatives of nobles and townspeople, presides at the Model Parliament.

But Parliament's power continued to grow. In the 1300s, Parliament divided into two **houses**. The representatives from the towns and cities formed their own section that became known as the House of Commons. The nobles became the House of Lords. The king and Parliament continued to struggle over power. Sometimes Parliament won the fight, and other times the king was stronger.

Parliament Today

Today, there is still a Parliament in London. Both houses of Parliament meet in the Palace of Westminster on the River Thames. The Houses of Parliament are among the most famous landmarks in London. There is still a **monarchy** in the country now known as the United Kingdom, or Britain, though it has very little power. So perhaps in the end, Parliament won!

British Minister of State for the Armed Forces, Andrew Robathan (right), gives U.S. Secretary of Defense Leon Panetta (left) a tour of the House of Lords.

Chapter 19
The Hundred Years' War

An Unstable Situation For many **generations** the rulers of England spoke French better than they spoke English. To make things even more confusing, many English nobles were required to be loyal to the king of France, too.

The Big Question

How did the decline of the feudal system change people's loyalties?

How could this be? Many years earlier, the French **ancestors** of a number of English nobles had received land from the king of France. As a result of the feudal system, this meant that they and their heirs continued to owe loyalty to the French king. This became a very big problem when the kings of England and France went to war.

Many English nobles had French ancestors.

Here was another complicated part of feudalism: these nobles and monarchs could marry only other monarchs and high-ranking nobles. As a result, kings and nobles around Europe were often related to one another. This caused great confusion when a king died. In fact, most wars were fought over the succession, or the order in which people took over the throne. Remember the Battle of Hastings?

In the early 1300s, the king of France died. He had no sons to take his place on the throne. However, the king of England, Edward III, was his nephew. Edward decided to take advantage of the relationship, and he claimed the throne of France. But nobody in France accepted his claim. Instead, Philip of Valois (val WAH), a French nobleman who was also related to the dead king, became King Philip VI of France. This conflict over the French throne triggered a war that became known as the Hundred Years' War.

A Misleading Name

The Hundred Years' War is a misleading name for a number of reasons. First of all, the Hundred Years' War lasted more than a hundred years. It lasted 116 years to be exact. Second, the Hundred Years' War was not a single war. It was several smaller wars fought between England and France. War did not go on all the time during the 116 years from 1337 to 1453. There were **truces** that lasted for up to twenty-five years. Even so, it is difficult to imagine two countries being at war with each other for so long.

> **Vocabulary**
>
> **truce,** n. an agreement to stop fighting

When the Hundred Years' War began, France was the richest and most powerful kingdom in Europe. It was rich in farming and grazing lands. French castles and churches were the envy of other kingdoms in Europe.

England, though not poor, was part of a small island with a harsher climate, fewer people, and less wealth than France. However, because of these age-old family ties, England also controlled lands in the western part of France. The English had no intention of giving up their claim to the French throne, and to these lands. In addition, one area of France known as Flanders was essential to England's economy. Indeed, one of the things that strengthened England's **economy** was the wool trade, in which Flanders played a part. The climate of England was challenging for growing crops but good for raising sheep. The wool from these sheep made lots of money. Highly skilled craftsmen and women in Flanders turned English wool into yarn that was used to make cloth. England needed to control Flanders. Not surprisingly, the people of Flanders were loyal to the English.

In military terms, it looked as though France had a big advantage. First, most of the war was fought in France, so the French were fighting on their home **territory**. Second, it was very expensive for the English to ship armored knights and horses across the English Channel to France. Finally, in most battles, the French had many more knights than the English.

> ## Vocabulary
>
> **economy,** n. the way a country manages its money and resources to produce, buy, and sell goods and services
>
> **territory,** n. an area of land

The Battle of Poitiers is just one of the many battles fought by the English and French during the Hundred Years' War.

But the English were stronger than they appeared. The English army made effective use of a powerful weapon called the **longbow**. With the longbow, archers could shoot arrows farther and with greater power. In fact, arrows shot from a longbow could cut through armor. This is one of the reasons why a war that the French thought they could win quickly turned into a war that went on for such a long time.

Bloody Battlefields

Thousands of soldiers died on each side during the Hundred Years' War. The use of the longbow took away the great advantage that armored knights previously had on the battlefield. English archers, when given the chance, easily defeated the French knights.

One of the most famous battles of the war was fought at the French town of Agincourt (AJ ihn kor). A large, powerful French army cornered a small English army. The French were sure of victory. The English were sure they would be defeated. But the superior tactics and powerful longbows of the English resulted in a terrible defeat for France.

The End of the War

Throughout history, wars have at times brought about change and innovation. This is because as each side tries to gain an advantage, they introduce new ideas and weapons. As a result, the way armies fight at the end of a war is often very different from the way they fought at the beginning. That certainly was the case in the Hundred Years' War. Remember how the longbow gave the English a military advantage? Well, the French never stopped trying to come up with better weapons of their own. Around 1400 they did.

England and France, 1337

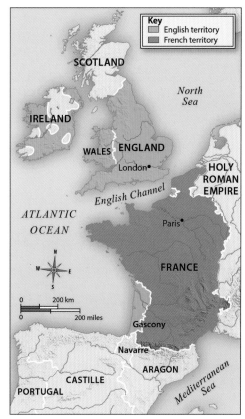

By the end of the Hundred Years' War, England had lost almost all of its lands in France.

The French developed **cannons** that were very powerful, easy to move around, and accurate. These cannons gave the French a big advantage. Finally the fighting stopped. The French had won. England was forced to give up almost all the territory it had controlled in France.

Vocabulary

cannon, n. a very large gun that fires iron balls

Effects of the War

The Hundred Years' War is more important for what happened to England and France than for the military results. Yes, France won the war and took territory from England. But both kingdoms were now changed forever.

France was terribly weakened from all the fighting on French land. English soldiers, far from home, had routinely looted French

The use of the cannon changed warfare in the Middle Ages.

towns, villages, and farms. English soldiers had held entire villages for ransom. They would capture a village, then threaten to burn it and kill everyone if people didn't give them money. All this looting and ransoming left France poorer than it had been before the war. It also left a feeling of hatred between the French and the English that lasted for hundreds of years.

The war had been very costly on the English side, too. Thousands of soldiers had died. Trade had suffered.

A Different World

If there were any real winners, they were the kings of both France and England. The deaths of so many knights weakened many noble families. The power of the noble barons was reduced, and kings in both countries became stronger.

The war also weakened the rule of feudalism. Towns and cities began to grow in size and power. Loyalty to feudal nobles declined, but a sense of loyalty to king and country grew.

This strong feeling for their country led to another big change for the English that affects us today. During the war the rulers of England and most educated and wealthy people stopped speaking French and began speaking English. Books and documents began to be written in English. People began to feel more united around a common language and culture.

History is always clearer when we look back on it than it is to the people living through it. Although the people didn't know it at the time, a new age was on the horizon.

Chapter 20
Joan of Arc

A Hero for the Ages You have read about great kings and warriors. Now you are going to read about a warrior who was certainly one of the greatest heroes of the entire Middle Ages. Her leadership **turned the tide** of battle in the Hundred Years' War. Her actions helped the French win a war that had gone on for so long.

The Big Question

Why do you think the story of Joan of Arc is still remembered today?

Yes, that's right, this great warrior was a woman—in fact a teenager. She was a simple peasant girl, not a well-educated woman of noble birth. She was not much bigger than most of you. But Joan of Arc became a giant in the history of the Middle Ages. Her story is still exciting to read more than 500 years after she lived.

Vocabulary

"turn the tide" (idiom) reverse the trend of events or the way things are going

Joan of Arc helped turn the tide in the Hundred Years' War.

Hope Returns

You have read about how the English won many battles against the French in the Hundred Years' War. France seemed to have all the advantages in the war, but these advantages were often of little use against the English. All the years of fighting and looting had left the French feeling hopeless and dispirited. It seemed as if they had lost the will to fight the English.

In battle after battle, ten to fifteen times as many French soldiers were killed as English soldiers. Both sides prepared for battle in a way that would seem strange to us today but was traditional in the Middle Ages. The French waited patiently on their horses while the English set up their barricades of pointed stacks and put all their archers into position. Then, when everyone was ready, the battle would begin. At that point the English would shower arrows on the advancing French horsemen. Shot from powerful longbows, the sharp arrows could pierce the French knights' thin sheets of armor. Most French knights never got close enough to use their swords on the English.

In the last decades of the war, though, the French looked for another way to fight the English. One of the reasons for this new sense of determination was inspired by a simple girl named Jeanne. In English we call her Joan. Joan believed that God had given her the mission of driving the English out of France and **restoring** the French king to the throne.

> **Vocabulary**
>
> **restore,** v. to return to the way things used to be

Visions and Voices

Joan grew up in a small village called Domrémy (dohm REH mee). When she was about thirteen years old, she began having visions and hearing voices. At first, these voices, which Joan believed to be the voices of God and the saints, simply told her to live a good life. As the years went by, however, she heard the voices more often. Finally, she understood that she was

Joan is usually portrayed wearing the clothing and armor of a soldier.

being told that God had chosen her to rescue the kingdom of France. Joan was seventeen years old.

Joan was stunned. She knew nothing about war or politics. Yet the voices continued. After the village of Domrémy was burned by the English, the voices became urgent and more specific. They told her that she should go to a large town about twelve miles from her home. There, Joan was told to ask the governor to arrange a meeting with the man who was next in line to be king, the **dauphin** (doh FAN).

> **Vocabulary**
>
> **dauphin,** n. the oldest son of the king of France; the male heir to the throne

The voices told Joan that her mission was to free the city of Orléans (or-lay AHN), which was under siege by the English, and to see the dauphin crowned king of France.

At first, the governor had no interest in meeting her. So Joan simply stood outside his castle, praying and explaining to people why she had come.

Joan soon had a small group of supporters. One of them, a young soldier, gave her a young man's clothes to put on. Someone else gave her a horse. Yet another person cut her hair for her. The governor finally agreed to meet her. At first he laughed at her, but later, for reasons no one really understands, he changed his mind. He gave her a sword and permission to go to the dauphin. He gave her an archer, a royal messenger, and three servants. Her friend, the young soldier, went as well.

A Victory at Orléans

Joan and her little band traveled through 350 miles of cold, flooded rivers and war-torn countryside. She was admitted into the grand hall of the castle where the dauphin was staying. It was filled with more than three hundred knights and many **courtiers** dressed in fine clothes. The dauphin stood among them.

> **Vocabulary**
>
> **courtier,** n. a noble who was part of the royal court and advised the ruler (king, queen or dauphin)

Legend has it that the dauphin was testing Joan by mingling with the crowd, but Joan surprised everyone by walking right up to him and kneeling before him. It may be that Joan had seen his picture before on coins or banners. Yet, it was impressive that a simple peasant girl could pick him out of such a crowd.

Joan was given a room in the castle, and she began to practice her fighting skills. A group of knights gathered around her. We can't explain how, but Joan soon had these famous warriors willing to do whatever she asked. All we can assume was that Joan's faith and her leadership inspired others to follow her. With an army of some three thousand to four thousand soldiers, Joan set off to Orléans.

The city had been under siege for nearly seven months. The English hadn't yet succeeded in capturing the city, but the French forces were becoming weak. As Joan rode through Orléans on the night of her arrival, townspeople carrying torches pressed around her. Rumors had spread through France that a young woman dressed as a boy had been sent by God to save them from the English.

Joan was eager to battle the English, but the French commander urged her to be patient. Joan agreed, but a few days later things changed. Joan urged the French commander to take action. "In God's name," she said, "my counsel [advisor] has told me I must attack the English." Her voices had spoken to her. She rode down to the gates of the city, where she found wounded French soldiers retreating from the English forces. When the French soldiers saw Joan on her horse, waving her white banner, they were **revived**. They turned around and headed back toward the English with such a surge of force that the English began to retreat.

> **Vocabulary**
> ....
> **revive,** v. to return to strength; to "bring back to life"

Joan predicted that she would be wounded, but she fought without a helmet so that her soldiers could see her. An arrow pierced her neck. She almost fainted with pain, but a few hours later she returned to the fight. After three days of fighting, the English were finally driven out of Orléans. The war was not over, but for the first time it seemed that the English might be defeated.

The people of Orléans cheered the victorious Joan and her soldiers.

A Crown for a King

Now Joan devoted herself to the next part of her mission. She returned to the dauphin and convinced him to travel to Reims (reemz). This was the city where French kings had been crowned for hundreds of years. The problem was that Reims was controlled by the Burgundians (bur GUN-dee unz), who were on the side of the English. When Joan arrived, however, the residents of the city had a change of heart. They cheered for the dauphin. The Burgundian army quietly slipped out of town, and the dauphin was crowned Charles VII, king of France. Joan was at the peak of her glory.

Politics and Prison

If the story of Joan of Arc were a fairy tale, she and King Charles VII would defeat the English and live happily ever after. In real life, politics entered the story.

Once he was crowned, the king began making deals behind Joan's back. Joan simply wanted to keep fighting until the English were driven out of France. But the king made deals with the Burgundians and the English without telling Joan.

In 1430, Joan was captured by Burgundian soldiers, who then handed her over to the English.

Trial and Death

Joan was thrown into prison. Because she claimed to hear the voice of God and the voices of saints, Joan had to **stand trial** for heresy. Heresy is the crime of going against the teachings of the Church. To prove this crime, Joan's enemies needed to find some people who were willing to repeat gossip or spread rumors. It took some time, but finally some ambitious churchmen stepped forward. They did not really know Joan but were eager to please the bishop and the English. Day after day they questioned her. They focused most of their questions on the voices that Joan claimed to hear and on the fact that she wore men's clothing. For a woman to wear men's clothing was a serious crime.

Vocabulary

"stand trial" (idiom) be judged guilty or innocent in a court of law

Joan answered their questions simply and truthfully. It was hard to make much of a case against her. But after weeks of questioning and accusations, her enemies succeeded, and the court sentenced her to death.

France Succeeds

Although Joan was executed in the year 1431, the tide of the war had turned. The French succeeded in driving the English out of all their territories except the city of Calais.

Twenty years after Joan's death, the Church investigated her trial. After a complete review of the evidence, it was decided that the trial had been unfair. It was too late to help Joan, and no one involved in the unfair trial was ever punished. But Joan's reputation as a great hero was secure. For hundreds of years, writers and artists have told her story in poems, plays, painting, and statues. In 1920, the Church declared the simple peasant girl a saint.

This statue of heroic Joan of Arc is in London's Westminster Cathedral.

Chapter 21
The Black Death

A Terrible Way to Die Imagine that you are a ten-year-old child living in Florence, Italy, in the year 1348. You have been sent by your parents to a nearby market. As you wander about the busy marketplace, you overhear people talking. "It started in Sicily," one man says.

The Big Question

Why do you think having a smaller population in Europe helped improve working conditions for serfs, as well as weaken the feudal system?

"No, no," says another man, "it started in the East. The Tartars began it."

The first man waves his hand impatiently. "No matter where it started, it's killed most of Sicily, and now it's coming here."

What on earth are these people talking about? You pull on the jacket sleeve of one of the men. "Sir, sir," you ask. "What are you talking about?"

The two men glance at one another. The man in the jacket turns and looks at you with stern eyes. "It's the Black Death, child. It's coming. Now run home and tell your parents to get you and your brothers and sisters out of town."

People in the markets of Florence in 1348 would likely have discussed the Black Death.

Before much time had passed, you would learn a great deal more about the Black Death. All around you, people would die. Some would die very quickly, almost as though they were poisoned. Others would linger for three days or even for six, most developing ugly growths in their armpits. Large red and black spots would appear on their skin. Some would fall into a deep sleep.

Nowhere to Run, Nowhere to Hide

The man who feared the worst turned out to be right. The Black Death did come to Florence, and it killed more than half the people in the city.

This **plague** seems to have started in Asia in the 1320s. It is thought to have been carried by fleas nesting in the fur of **rodents**. These rodents crawled onto ships and brought the infected fleas with them to cities in southern Europe, especially to Sicily, in 1347. The next year it spread inland and around the Mediterranean. It attacked southern England, France, Italy, Spain, northern Africa, and Greece. There was still hope that it would stop, but eventually it found its way into northern Germany, northern England, Scotland, and the Scandinavian countries of Norway and Sweden. The Black Death reached all the way to Iceland and Greenland.

> ### Vocabulary
>
> **plague,** n. a highly contagious, usually fatal disease that affects large numbers of people
>
> **rodent,** n. a gnawing mammal, such as a rat, mouse, gerbil, or hamster

Some people thought the Black Death was a punishment for sins. They hit themselves with whips to try to make up for anything they had done wrong.

Disappearing Villages

The worst outbreak of the Black Death lasted for four years, between 1347 and 1350. When it was over, Europe was a very different place. It is estimated that about 25 million people, or one-third of the population, died of the plague.

Some areas were hit harder than others. In some regions as many as two-thirds of the population died. In England alone, about a thousand villages disappeared as a result of the plague. In some places there were not enough people remaining to bury the dead. People who survived moved to larger towns.

The Spread of the Black Death

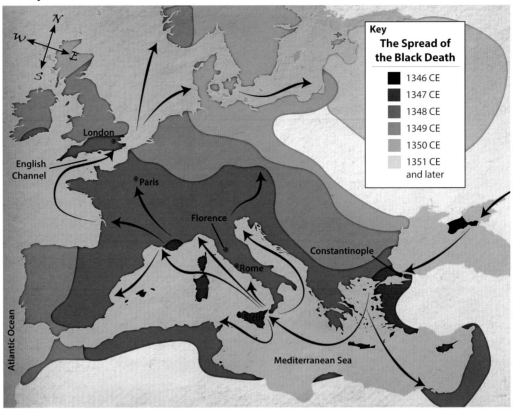

The Black Death was so severe that in many places there were not enough coffins and, often, no one to conduct funeral services. It took about 250 years for the population of Europe to recover.

Long-Term Effects

Once the Black Death had passed, people started to rebuild and restore their communities. Because so many people had died, there was a labor shortage. Now serfs could bargain for better working conditions. Over time, serfs were able to buy their own land as well as their freedom. Within a hundred years, serfdom had almost entirely disappeared from western Europe.

The shortage of workers also inspired people to try to invent **labor-saving**

> **Vocabulary**
>
> **labor-saving,** adj. requiring a smaller amount of work or effort to get the same job done

devices. New types of water mills and windmills were invented. Efforts to understand the horrors of the Black Death and to prevent it from happening encouraged an interest in science and medicine. Over time, cities developed more organized public-health systems that helped them deal with the outbreak of diseases in general. Governments took more responsibility for founding hospitals.

The End of the Middle Ages

Remember how the Hundred Years' War helped weaken feudalism? The Black Death also helped weaken feudal ties. Instead of feudal lords, kings and their administrators helped keep law and order.

By 1500, Europe had changed quite a lot. City and town governments had gained more influence. Knights and armor were on the way out; cannons and cannonballs were on the way in. Universities were being established so that more people could study law, medicine, and other subjects. In Italy, educated people had begun to look back to the writings and art produced by ancient Greeks and Romans thousands of years earlier. The movement we call the **Renaissance** had begun. There were more cities and more trade. Some traders began to look for more ways to trade with people outside of

> **Vocabulary**
> ....
> **Renaissance,** n.
> a trend in reviving classical art and literature in Europe, beginning in the 1300s

Europe. They ventured as far as Africa and then to the Americas. With the dawn of these new times, the world of feudalism, lords, vassals, serfs, knights, and courtly love slowly faded away.

Glossary

A

abbess, n. the leader of a convent (89)

abbot, n. the leader of a monastery (29)

administrator, n. a person responsible for carrying out the day-to-day workings of an organization (106)

alliance, n. a partnership of different countries, organizations, or people who agree to work together (41)

ancestor, n. a relative who lived a long time ago (136)

annul, v. to cancel; to make no longer legal or true (119)

> **annulment, n.** the act of making a marriage no longer legal or valid

apprentice n. a person who is learning a trade from a master craftsman (82)

aqueduct, n. a raised canal that carries water from one place to another (12)

armor, n. metal outer covering worn to protect the body in battle (64)

artisan, n. a person with a certain skill in making things (13)

B

baron, n. a lord; a lower rank in the British nobility (126)

bishop, n. a high-ranking member of the church in some Christian religions (16)

blessing, n. a prayer of support, protection, and approval for someone (39)

boundary, n. the edge of a country or of an area; its outside limits (4)

C

cannon, n. a very large gun that fires iron balls (142)

cathedral, n. the bishop's church; any large and important church (38)

charter, n. a document given by a ruler to a group of people that allows them to elect their own government officials (84)

Christian, adj. related to beliefs based on the teachings of Jesus of Nazareth (18)

> **Christianity, n.** a religion based on the teachings of Jesus of Nazareth
>
> **Christian, n.** a person who believes that Jesus of Nazareth is God

circuit, n. an area or district through which a judge travels to hold court sessions (130)

citizen, n. in the Middle Ages, a skilled tradesman, artisan, or important merchant who was a resident of a city (132)

"claim to the throne," (idiom), the right to be the ruler (94)

"Code of Chivalry," (phrase), a set of rules of behavior for knights (70)

composer, n. a person who writes music (89)

conqueror, n. a person who takes control of a territory after an invasion (96)

> **conquer, v.** to defeat or take control by force
>
> **conquest, n.** a defeat (97)

convent, n. a community of nuns, or women who live a simple, religious life (29)

convert, v. to change religious beliefs; to switch from one religion to another (18)

council, n. a group of people organized to govern (130)

court, n. a place where legal matters are presented and decisions made about disputes or people who have broken the law (106)

courtier, n. a noble who was part of the royal court and advised the ruler (king, queen, or dauphin) (148)

crown, v. to put a crown on someone's head in a ceremony, making him or her king, queen, or emperor of a certain area (39)

crusade, n. religious wars during the Middle Ages in which Christians from Europe attempted to recover territory from Muslims in the Middle East (122)

custom, n. a tradition, or way of doing something, that belongs to a particular society, place, or time (18)

D

dauphin, n. the oldest son of the king of France; the male heir to the throne (147)

decline, n. gradual loss of importance and power (4)

democracy, n. a form of government in which people choose their leaders; a country with this form of government (129)

devotion, n. strong loyalty to a cause or belief (89)

devout, adj. showing deep religious feelings (110)

duchess, n. a female noble who is the wife or widow of a duke or who rules a small territory herself (116)

duke, n. a male noble who rules a small territory (92)

> **duchy, n.** a territory or region ruled by a duke or duchess

dynasty, n. a series of rulers who are all from the same family (107)

E

economy, n. the way a country manages its money and resources to produce, buy, and sell goods and services (139)

empire, n. a group of countries controlled by a single authority (2)

estate, n. an area of land or property (50)

excommunication, n. a punishment given by a high-ranking religious official saying that a person can no longer be part of the Church (113)

F

feud, n. a long and bitter argument (112)

feudalism, n. a system of government in which land is exchanged for loyalty and services (42)

fief, n. a plot of land exchanged for loyalty to a ruler (44)

fortress, n. a fort; a place that has been built to be strong enough to provide protection (58)

G

generation, n. all the people born and living at around the same time, equal to about twenty-five years (136)

government, n. a small group of people who have the authority to make rules for a much larger group, such as people living in a particular city, region, or country (105)

guild, n. a group of businessmen who control a certain craft (82)

H

healer, n. a person who cures the sick (76)

hearth, n. the bottom of a fireplace (75)

heir, n. a person who will legally receive the property of someone who dies; the person who will become king or queen after the current king or queen dies or steps down (20)

"hold court," (idiom), be the center of attention, be surrounded by people who want to talk, listen, and entertain (120)

"holy ceremony," (phrase), a religious act or ritual performed according to tradition (22)

hostage, n. a person taken by force and held prisoner, often later exchanged for money or other demands (126)

house, n. a building in which people meet for a particular activity; a chamber of Parliament (134)

hygiene, n. cleanliness (88)

I

invader, n. a person or group that comes into a country by force (4)

J

journeyman, n. a guild member who is considered qualified to work for wages in a particular trade (83)

jousting, n. a tournament in which two opponents on horseback fight with lances (70)

jury, n. a group of people who listen to information presented during a trial in a court and make decisions about whether someone is guilty or innocent (107)

K

knight, n. a soldier on horseback who serves a king or other ruler (42)

L

labor-saving, adj. requiring a smaller amount of work or effort to get the same job done (158)

lance, n. a long weapon with a pointed metal tip, used by horsemen when charging an opponent (67)

livestock, n. the animals kept on a farm (75)

longbow, n. a large bow pulled by hand and used to shoot a long, feathered arrow (140)

loophole, n. a way around a law or rule (111)

lord, n. a person with power and influence who controls land given to him by a king (42)

M

manage, v. to lead and direct; to run something, such as a project or business (36)

management, n. the act of leading and directing

manager, n. a person who leads and directs something, such as a project or business (40)

manor, n. a large country house and its surrounding land (50)

manuscript, n. a book or document written by hand (32)

Mass, n. the name for the religious ceremony in which Catholics celebrate their relationship with God (38)

masterpiece, n. a perfect example of a finished product of some craft (83)

medieval, adj. relating to the Middle Ages in Europe (44)

merchant, n. a person who buys and sells goods to earn money (13)

missionary, n. a person on a journey for the purpose of spreading a particular religious belief (30)

> **mission, n.** a task or duty in which one strongly believes

monarch, n. a king or queen (135)

monastery, n. a place where a community of monks live (27)

monk, n. a member of a religious community of men who promise to live very simply (26)

N

nobility, n. powerful families that held fiefs and titles (42)

nutrient, n. something that provides what is needed to grow and live (54)

P

parliament, n. a group made up of representatives and the monarch, who make the laws for a country; a term used especially in England to describe the lawmaking part of the government (133)

peasant, n. a person of low social rank, usually a farmer or unskilled worker (72)

pilgrimage, n. a journey undertaken for a religious purpose (115)

plague, n. a highly contagious, usually fatal disease that affects large numbers of people (156)

politics, n. the activities of a leader or ruler running a government (94)

proposal, n. an offer of marriage (119)

R

ransom, n. payment for the release of a prisoner (122)

record, n. evidence of events from the past (97)

reform, n. an improvement (123)

religious, adj. relating to beliefs about God or several gods to explain how the world started, why things happen, and how people should live in the world (88)

Renaissance, n. a trend in reviving classical art and literature in Europe, beginning in the 1300s (159)

representative, n. a person in government who makes decisions and votes on behalf of a group of people (132)

restore, v. to return to the way things used to be (146)

revive, v. to return to strength; to "bring back to life" (149)

right, n. a legal promise (129)

rodent, n. a gnawing mammal, such as a rat, mouse, gerbil, or hamster (156)

S

sack, v. to destroy and steal things in a city or building, usually with an army (5)

scholar, n. a person with special knowledge about a subject (14)

scripture, n. the sacred writings of a religion (29)

security, n. safety, freedom from danger (74)

self-sufficient, adj. needing no help from others to live or survive (48)

serf, n. a person living on a feudal estate who was required to work for the lord of the manor; a serf could not choose to leave the estate, but was required to stay and work the land as the lord demanded; a peasant who is not free (50)

shrine, n. a place considered holy because it is associated with a religious person or saint (115)

siege, n. a battle strategy in which enemy soldiers surround a building or place so that those under attack cannot receive supplies; blockade (61)

"stand trial," (idiom), be judged guilty or innocent in a court of law (151)

successor, n. a person who becomes king, queen, or leader after the recent leader's death (104)

T

tapestry, n. a handwoven wall hanging that may depict people and/or a scene (63)

tax, n. money collected from citizens by the government (99)

territory, n. an area of land (139)

tournament, n. a series of contests among more than two competitors competing for an overall prize (68)

trade, n. buying and selling goods among different peoples (13)

trial, n. a legal process used to decide if a person is guilty or innocent (106)

troubadour, n. a person who writes and performs poetry set to music (71)

truce, n. an agreement to stop fighting (138)

"turn the tide," (idiom), reverse the trend of events or the way things are going (144)

U

uncivilized, adj. not advanced socially or culturally (5)

uncultured, adj. showing poor manners and bad taste; crude (5)

university, n. a school where advanced learning is taught (91)

V

vassal, n. a person who receives land from a ruler and in return promises to fight for the ruler (44)

version, n. a draft; a form of something, like a document, that is different from other forms of the same thing (128)

victor, n. a person who defeats an opponent or enemy; winner (18)

village, n. a group of houses and buildings, smaller than a town, in a rural area (50)

vision, n. an image in one's mind or imagination that others cannot see (90)

W

warfare, n. the activity of fighting a war (63)

well, n. a hole dug deep into the ground to get water (60)